LOSING SANTHIA

LIFE AND LOSS IN THE STRUGGLE FOR TAMIL EELAM

Ben Hillier

"This elegantly written essay is an excellent background to the ongoing Eelam Tamil struggle. Mixing the history of military battles with the history of social change and personal stories makes it an absorbing read. Ben Hillier gives an insightful account of the struggle and shows sensitivity towards the struggling people – a rare quality among writers of politics in today's neoliberal world. *Losing Santhia* captures the loss of an individual and symbolises the loss of a people. For me the title perhaps more importantly alludes to the loss of a new kind of Tamil woman who was emerging in the now destroyed de facto state of Tamil Eelam."

– N. Malathy, author of *A fleeting moment in my country: the last years of the LTTE de-facto state* and *Tamil female civil space: its evolution and decline in Tamil Eelam*

"A compelling account of the struggle for independence waged by the Tamil people. Importantly, Ben Hillier provides significant insights into how the struggle was brought to an end through global actors pursuing their own interests. He invites readers to evaluate many of the criticisms levelled against the Liberation Tigers of Tamil Eelam in the light of ground realities, particularly the demand to live up to international standards without institutional preconditions."

– Ana Pararajasingham, editor of *Sri Lanka: 60 years of "independence" and beyond* and author of *Sri Lanka's endangered peace process and the way forward*

"The smell of death lingers over the pages of Ben Hillier's *Losing Santhia*. It is confronting but necessary to read what happened when tens of thousands of Tamils were corralled on the Mullivaikal beach in so-called no fire zones. Hillier provides an honest appraisal of what happened to members of the Tigers in this period. While the setback for Tamil self-determination was massive, there is also a positive story from the heart of the struggle. And personal stories of love and happiness from the front line bring hope to the fore. The essay ends with the critical question – can the progressive left forces in Sri Lanka forge a common purpose?"

– Lee Rhiannon, former Australian Greens federal senator

"An important and moving contribution. This is a story of loss, not only of a person, and perhaps more than a hundred thousand others, but of a dream crushed, for the moment at least, in dreadful pain and suffering. Santhia's story brings us a glimpse of that dream and shows us another side of the often demonised Tigers. In so doing, it can help build solidarity with refugees and asylum seekers from Sri Lanka and other war-torn countries and with the ongoing struggle to build a better world."
– Helen Jarvis, vice president of the Permanent Peoples' Tribunal and former head of the Victims Support Section of the Extraordinary Chambers in the Courts of Cambodia

"A remarkable essay. Not only does Ben Hillier provide a startlingly lyrical account of such terrible events, his balanced assessment of the Tamil Tigers' choice of a military strategy is of considerable interest in these days of resistance to authoritarian and exploitative corporate state regimes. The inclusion of the seminal document on liberation and self-determination by Tiger theorist Anton Balasingham provides essential background reading. All those interested in contemporary struggles for self-determination should read this."
– Gill H. Boehringer, former head, now honorary senior research associate, Macquarie University Law School and co-chair of the Monitoring Committee on Attacks on Lawyers, International Association of People's Lawyers

"A fascinating account. *Losing Santhia* interweaves the stories of an individual, an organisation and a nation, all pursuing liberation. The stories are tragic, ending in a defeat that resulted from a flawed strategy and the combined power of domestic and international forces that imposed or supported oppression. But they are also stories of heroism and hope – because oppression inevitably gives rise to resistance and resistance is not inevitably doomed."
– Rick Kuhn, honorary associate professor in sociology, Australian National University

First published 2019 by Interventions Inc

All proceeds from the sale of this book go to the Tamil Refugee Council in Australia.

Interventions is a not-for-profit, independent left wing book publisher. For further information:
interventions.org.au
interventionspublications@gmail.com
Trades Hall Suite 68
54 Victoria Street
Carlton VIC 3053

Design and layout by Viktoria Ivanova
All poems republished with permission from Tamil Tiger Women Writing, translated and edited by N. Malathy
Illustrations by Henri Eberhard

Author: Hillier, Ben

Title: Losing Santhia: Life and loss in the struggle for Tamil Eelam
With Anton Balasingham Liberation Tigers and Tamil Eelam freedom struggle

ISBN: 978-0-9945378-6-7: Paperback

© Ben Hillier 2019

The moral rights of the author have been asserted.
All rights reserved. Except as permitted under the Australian Copyright Act 1968 (for example, a fair dealing for the purposes of study, research, criticism or review), no part of this book may be reproduced, stored in a retrieval system, communicated or transmitted in any form or by any means without prior written permission.

All inquiries should be made to the author.

A catalogue record for this book is available from the National Library of Australia

NATIONAL LIBRARY OF AUSTRALIA

LOSING SANTHIA

LIFE AND LOSS IN THE STRUGGLE FOR TAMIL EELAM

Ben Hillier

With Anton Balasingham's *Liberation Tigers and Tamil Eelam freedom struggle*

INTERVENTIONS
MELBOURNE

Early dawn awaits round the corner
Bird songs welcome the new dawn
Trees come alive shaking off dew
Dry bushes too look afresh
Sound of explosions nearby
Bombs eager to embrace us.

Comrade next to me – her hand
That held the gun falls still
Her blood paints new picture on the soil
The young daughter's lifeless body
Fills our fiery eyes with tears
Her gun now blasts in another hand
Our pace goes up
The explosions still heard afar.

The land is silent
Grieving for her young daughter
Crushed trees, wingless birds
And the burning bushes
Stand up straight with their injuries
Their marks of freedom struggle.
On the soil muddied by blood
Our feet speed towards the goal
Memory filled eyes await
The next dawn.

– Barathy, "Rise up for the new dawn"

With thanks to Aran, Vasanthan, Jessica, Umesh, Malathy, the doctor, the professor, the driver, the translator and Simon, and to Viktoria for design, Henri for illustrations and Roger Parton for the use of two photos of Tamil Tigers from the early 1990s (rogerparton.com). Poems throughout the text are republished with permission from *Tamil Tiger Women Writing*, translated and edited by N. Malathy, available online.

Dedicated to those who risked much to tell their stories and to those who tried their best to win liberation.

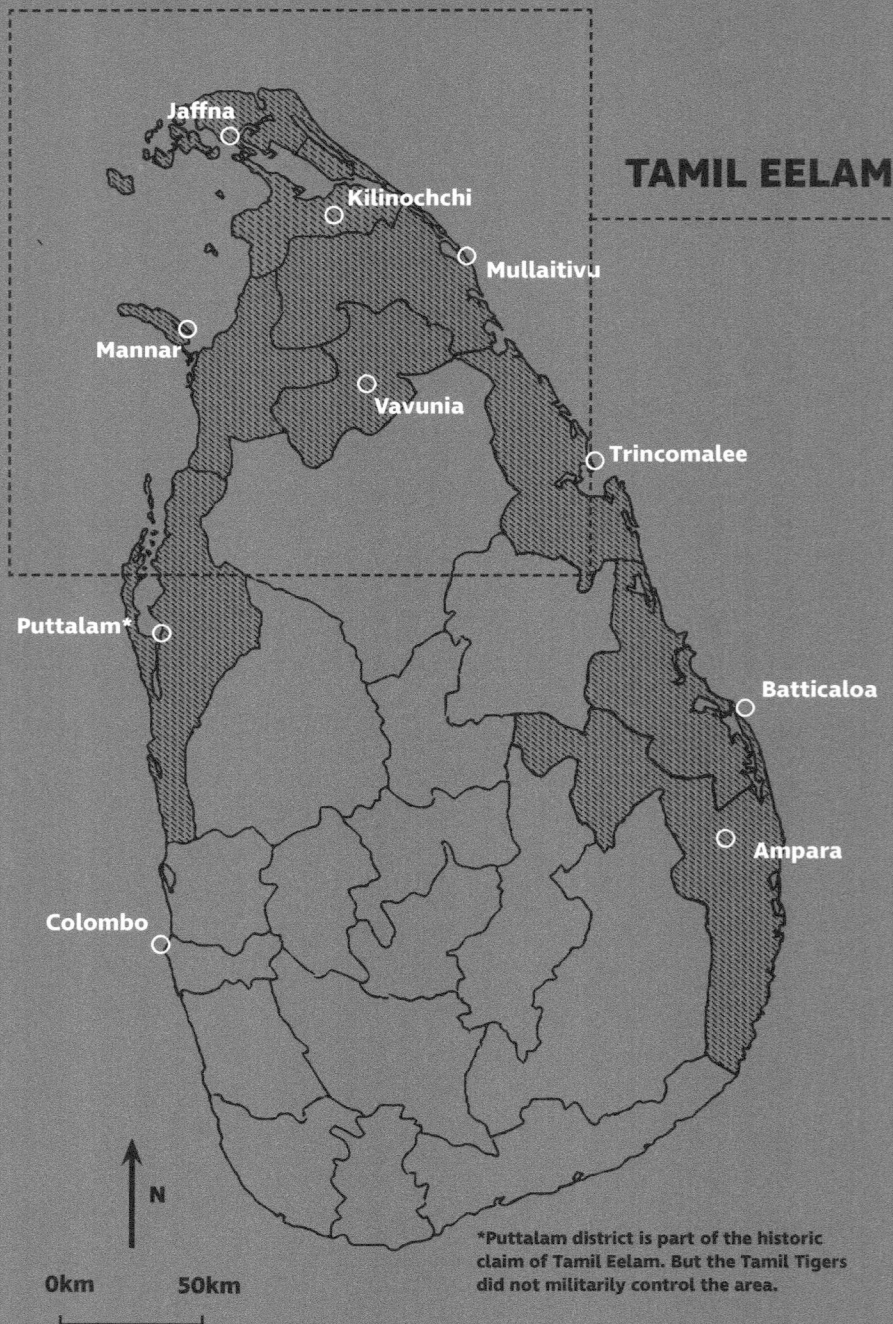

Jaffna

TAMIL EELAM

Kilinochchi

Mullaitivu

Mannar

Vavunia

Trincomalee

Puttalam*

Batticaloa

Colombo

Ampara

N

0km   50km

*Puttalam district is part of the historic
claim of Tamil Eelam. But the Tamil Tigers
did not militarily control the area.

VANNI AND JAFFNA

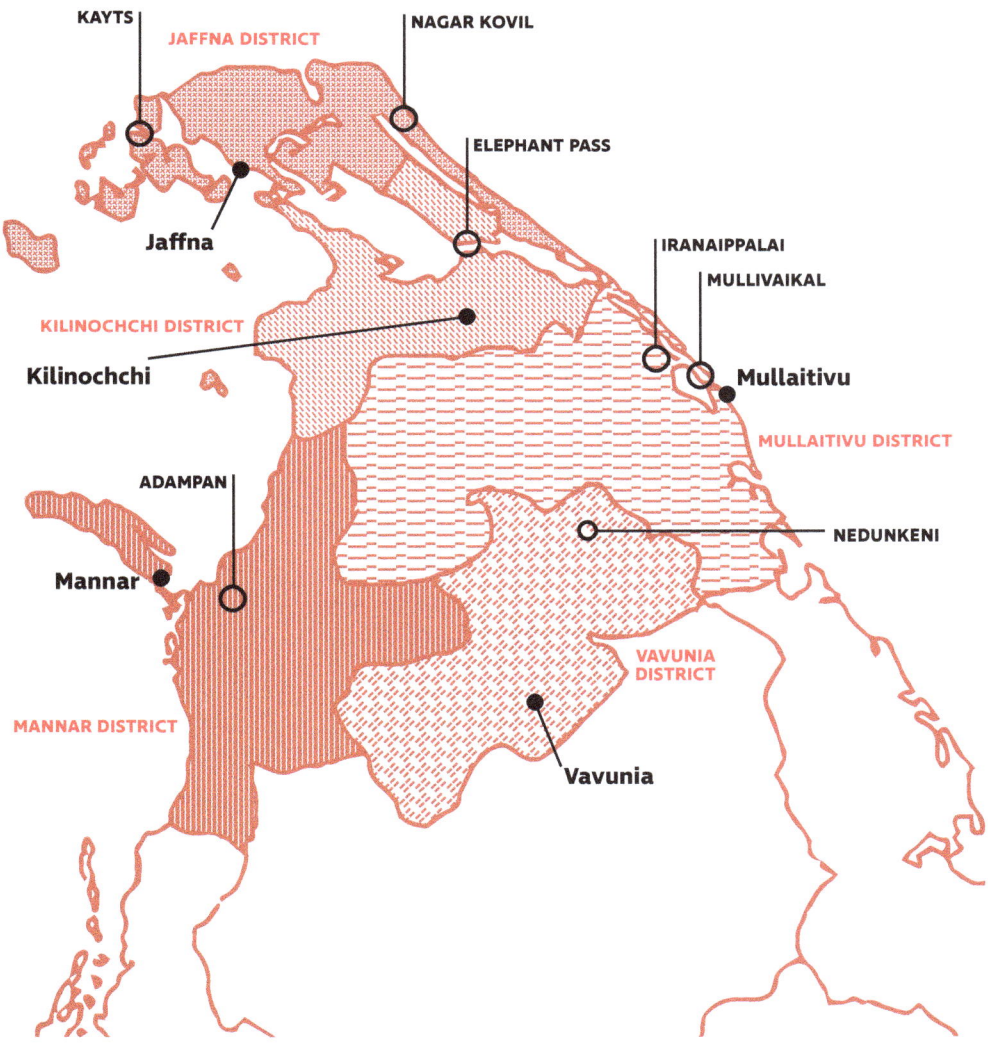

KAYTS

JAFFNA DISTRICT

NAGAR KOVIL

ELEPHANT PASS

Jaffna

IRANAIPPALAI

MULLIVAIKAL

KILINOCHCHI DISTRICT

Kilinochchi

Mullaitivu

MULLAITIVU DISTRICT

ADAMPAN

NEDUNKENI

Mannar

VAVUNIA
DISTRICT

MANNAR DISTRICT

Vavunia

CONTENTS

FOREWORD

On a small stretch of sand in north-eastern Sri Lanka in 2009, the military launched a genocidal offensive against the island's Tamils. The government told the world that it was rescuing civilians from the grip of the Liberation Tigers of Tamil Eelam. It was a lie. The Tigers had waged a three-decade-long national liberation war with mass support. Desperate to wipe out the movement, the Sri Lankan armed forces indiscriminately bombed the entire population. Tens of thousands were killed in an act of premeditated extermination. The LTTE was militarily defeated; most of its leadership and cadres wiped out. But some survived. Santhia was one. After the war, she and her infant son fled Sri Lanka to Tamil Nadu, the southernmost state of India. They tried to reach Australia but were stranded in Indonesia. Santhia died in a Jakarta hospital in October 2017 aged just forty-two.

Sponsored by the Tamil Refugee Council, Ben Hillier travelled to Indonesia and Sri Lanka after Santhia's death to piece together her life. What follows is not a biography, however. Santhia's story is extraordinary, but it does not stand out as more worthy of telling than those of the tens of thousands of others who fought and died in the liberation war or who were scattered to the four corners of the earth as political exiles. So while Santhia is the subject of the title of this piece, her life appears only in fragments during the broader narrative of the rise and fall of the Tigers and as an individual expression of a nation's fight for liberation.

The essay is paired with a seminal document, *Liberation Tigers and*

Tamil Eelam freedom struggle, written in 1983 by Anton Balasingham on behalf of the Tigers' political committee. Balasingham, who died in 2006, was the organisation's chief negotiator. His piece provides an insight into the thinking of the leadership and is essential background to the origins of the war.

LOSING SANTHIA

EXILE

We wanted to walk
Holding your hands
Ever present death
Has become cheap
Your price keeps going up
Elsewhere you go cheap
We paid by heaps – but
We only get bullets

To the bullets we say
You cannot swallow freedom
You cannot put out that fire – so
Leave the brave souls
And surrender to the
Enemies of humanity.

– Kasthoori, "Oh Freedom ..."

6

Graha Maria Annai Velangkanni, Medan, northern Sumatra

Half a dozen young men,

ex-soldiers dedicated to national defence, sit on plastic chairs beneath the seven-storey Marian Shrine of Graha Maria Annai Velangkanni (Our Lady of Good Health), an imposing Indo-Mughal-styled Catholic temple in Medan, northern Sumatra. In turn, each bares his wounds. A foot, mangled bones almost protruding through the skin; welts in a

"We are stateless.
I haven't seen my
husband in a decade.
Our child doesn't
know his father."

"Our life is finished."

forearm and a chest where bullets tore through; an eye white blind. Shrapnel remains embedded in their bodies almost a decade after the conflict's terrible end. They once were cadres of the Liberation Tigers of Tamil Eelam. Several resisted the final Sri Lankan military offensives in their homeland. But there are no war stories today.

"Our life is finished." Only one can speak English; he relays their collective sentiments. "We are hoping for our children's future. We have no country … but we are human, and we'd like to be living like a human. We suffered in Sri Lanka. Now we suffer in Indonesia." These Tamils fled, only to be marooned on the western edge of this vast archipelago – their injuries never properly treated; their situation an open sore. Several hundred are here, in Indonesia's fourth largest city. Perhaps one hundred, maybe more, have been granted refugee status. Yet all remain in limbo. Indonesia is not a signatory to the United Nations refugee convention. While UN-approved people are released from detention, they have few

rights and are restricted in their movements. "We can't go out at night. We can't go to the beachside. We can't work. We can't drive the car. We are under the control of immigration", they say. "Still we hope the UNHCR [the UN refugee agency] or other countries will help us, because we can't go back to Sri Lanka. The problem is the government … We have been living out of the country for seven years, nine years. [If] we go there, what can we do? The government won't give us a chance to live … We can't go back."

Across Tamil Eelam – the traditional homelands of the Tamil-speaking peoples in the north and east of Sri Lanka – in south and south-east Asian refugee camps and in the diaspora, Tamil activists are in political disarray. Hundreds of thousands are stateless or permanent émigrés. Millions lack national rights. The routing of the Tigers has disorganised and demoralised a nation, the majority of whom previously were cohered around the liberation struggle. "Those who fought for the movement are suffering

10

Santhia

the most [under] local authorities, despite having contributed something for people's liberation", a destitute former LTTE cadre says over Skype from a nearby country. "There are people here who lost their families in the war and are now fighting for their lives because of their injuries. We're all living in fear. We can't even go to the local shop because there is a crackdown here. We are stateless. I haven't seen my husband in a decade. Our child doesn't know his father. That is the situation for many families."

The LTTE was one of the most formidable national liberation insurgencies of the post-World War Two era. From guerrilla origins in the early 1970s, the organisation in the first decade of the twentieth century established a de facto state, repelling the Sri Lankan military, police and security forces. It was a bulwark against state-sponsored colonisation schemes for Sinhalese Buddhists, the majority ethnic group from the south and centre of the island. But the end, when it came in 2009, was devastating. Almost all the leadership and leading cadres, along with tens of thousands of civilians, were wiped out.

A decade later, the casualties continue to mount. Santhia was forty-two when her kidneys failed. She succumbed on 1 October 2017 in a Jakarta hospital, having been stranded in Indonesia for more than seven years. Despite being acknowledged as a refugee, she could not secure resettlement in another country. Like her brother and many teenagers who resisted the Sinhalese-chauvinist state, Santhia joined the Tigers young. "Santhia was in charge of Black Tigers administration and logistics and the Imran Pandian women's brigade administration and logistics", a former comrade says. "She was in the eighteenth batch of the women's wing, which would have been [inducted] in 1992 or 1993." The Black Tigers was a commando force. In the Imran Pandian division, she reported to Gaddafi (an assumed name), former bodyguard of Tiger leader Velupillai Prabhakaran.

In the mid-2000s, Santhia married Kumaran, a senior military commander and nephew of Balraj, one of the highest ranking LTTE leaders. She moved to Kilinochchi, the administrative capital of the Tamil state in the northern Vanni – the mainland area below the Jaffna peninsula, stretching from Mannar on the west coast to Mullaitivu district in the east and south to Vavunia. When, in 2006, the fourth Eelam war erupted (the previous wars are generally dated 1983-87, 1990-95 and 1995-2002) after peace negotiations broke down, the Sri Lankan government vowed to liquidate the resistance. All hell was unleashed in the north. Kumaran and Santhia's brother disappeared in the 2009 final assaults on Mullaitivu, the LTTE's military stronghold. Santhia survived and fled with her young son to Tamil Nadu, southern India, before trying to reach Australia. They and about one hundred others, including fifteen children, spent sixty days at sea in the northern Indian Ocean. It was late 2010.

Several men here in Medan were on the same boat. "She didn't know if her husband was living or dead. She was thinking about this the whole time", one of them says. "She left India mainly because she wanted to save her son." Diesel and supplies ran out fifteen days after they launched. The next forty-five days were spent drifting, fishing and collecting rainwater. They traded money and jewellery with some fishermen. Then the GPS failed, leaving the vessel directionless, they say. Eventually, the asylum seekers landed on a western-Indonesian island. The navy picked them up a week later and placed them in immigration detention, with families housed in a free camp near Jakarta. Santhia was later granted refugee status and transferred to the Medan immigration centre. "In 2014, the UNHCR [initiated] the resettlement process to America", a friend says. "She finished the American embassy interview and finished the medical [evaluation], too. Then, the IOM [International Organization for Migration] brought [her back] to Jakarta. She hoped she could go to America ... But she was rejected."

Midday hymns from an upstairs choir echo in the forecourt.

"She saw the military
kill Tamil people.
That's why she wanted
to join the LTTE."

Decorating the school, Medan

The men volunteer here. Helped by pastor James Bharataputra, the visionary behind the grand design of the Graha Maria Annai Velangkanni, they are building a school for Tamil children in a nearby building owned by the parish. The youngsters have decorated the plywood walls with crayon – mountains, oceans and beaches, waterfalls and flowers. But the resources are few; this is just getting off the ground. One adult volunteer is finishing off the touches of a Mickey Mouse painting at the entrance. In a back room of the church the following day, a relative sits quietly. "Santhia was very kind and very clever. She was a talented poet", she says. "She was very angry … And she saw the military kill Tamil people. That's why she wanted to join the LTTE."

Living stretches, empty and long
Kitchen smoke, taste of food
And the man's welfare – these
Determine or is it cursed as living.

The competence to send roots
To seek water in the rocks is wasted
As sandy surface roots of
Skyward looking colourful plants

Woman;
All that competence to achieve
Why this tragedy? Whose deception?
Asphyxiating masks of
Daughter, wife and mother,
The longings to throw the masks
Supressed into the unconscious.
Enough is enough – these staged facade
It is not wrong for woman to be woman.

Be not satisfied with the breeze
That comes through the window.
Learn the feat of breaking the lock.
Open the door and possess all.

Thinking freely and loving freedom
These are not crimes to fear.
Think yourself, love yourself.
The world should be yours.

– Thamilaval, "The world is yours ..."

CUBS

Tamil Tigers, Jaffna, early 1990s

Leaving the Jaffna peninsula for Mannar

Along the Pannai causeway

linking Jaffna peninsula with
Mandaitivu and Kayts islands,
egret, black-headed ibis and
Eurasian wigeon bathe in the
shallows of the Palk Strait, which
stretches to Tamil Nadu. "They
have no passport or visa", the
translator says. "But they have
more freedom than we do." Santhia spent part of her childhood
around here, in the surrounds of
the sky blue St Mary's church, one
of three Catholic congregations on

Kayts. The legacy of war is evident in abandoned and overgrown houses, some just skeletons of their former homeliness.

In nearby Jaffna town, sea-shells hang from a beam on Pakkiyawathy's veranda. They are supposed to bring good fortune. But like hundreds of thousands of others, her life has been repeated-ly disrupted by war. When the Sri Lankan military belted and retook Jaffna in 1995 after five years of Ti-ger rule, she fled occupied Kayts, heading south-east to Kilinochchi. Pakkiyawathy later returned to Jaffna, but after a few years again moved east, finding herself in Mullaitivu in 2008-09, where the genocidal slaughter reached its apogee. Today, she is settled in a small pink house with a calicut tile roof, a stone's throw from one of the city's many Hindu temples. In the front room, a portrait of Santhia sits on a polished wood cabinet. Pakkiyawathy is Santhia's aunt but was given the baby to raise – a gift and a responsibility. She speaks with love of a child who always shared her food, was a good student and a teacher to

St. church, Kayts

her friends. Was she rebellious? Stubborn? No. "When she was a teenager, she was still a child, always smiling and laughing", another relative says. Yet the military's intrusions took their toll.

Santhia was still in high school when she joined the Tigers, undergoing months of training in a rudimentary camp. "She went to school in the morning, came home, ate her favourite meal then left the house and joined them", Pakkiyawathy says with pride. The warm hospitality characteristic of this part of the world – creamy soda on a silver tray, invitations to eat – is served with absences difficult to digest. Her eyes, fastened to the questions, are dams holding back a deluge. Yet they breach. Rivers of anguish flow as she relates that scarcely a week separated the word of her adopted daughter's passing from the news of her own father's death.

— — —

What motivates someone to take up arms against the state? Perhaps a better question: what motivated tens of thousands to rise in war? That is best answered by leaders of the national liberation army. Anton Balasingham's *Liberation Tigers and Tamil Eelam freedom struggle*, written on behalf of the political committee of the LTTE, is included later for that purpose. But a couple of preliminary answers are appropriate.

First is the particularly virulent strain of Buddhist nationalism here. When the British relinquished colonial rule over the island, then called Ceylon, in 1948, it did so through a peaceful transfer enabling the Crown to retain influence within a political elite dominated by representatives drawn from the Buddhist Sinhalese majority. The lack of a unified independence movement meant that genuine unity was never realised between Sinhalese and Tamils. Divide and rule, central to the colonial structure of domination, continued to be the preeminent post-colonial strategy of British imperialism and was welcomed by the newly-anointed Sinhalese rulers. Mirjam Weiberg-Salzmann from the University of

Münster in Germany notes the growing fundamentalism after independence, and an increasingly reactionary bond of religion, ethnicity and state power:

"Whereas in the 1940s only a small minority of monks had been politically active, in the 1950s monks from all the Nikayas (sects of the order) became involved … In the new history of Sri Lanka, the Tamils constituted a permanent and existential threat … The sangha [Buddhist clerical order] demanded active steps for the protection of Buddhism and attempted to institutionalise the traditional connection between religion and politics … The parliamentary elections of 1956 provided a large forum for the monks, which helped them spread their ideas. In the election campaign Tamils were branded parasites and the 'death knell' of the Buddhist Sinhalese, and hence a limited use of violence was supported … Sinhalese was declared the sole national language. From the 1960s 'Sinhalese' and 'Buddhist' became synonymous terms, and religious activities became a necessary criterion for qualification to a political post and an indispensable element of election propaganda. State and nation were henceforth defined by (1) Buddhism, and (2) Sinhala-ness."

This extreme form of Sinhalese-Buddhist nationalism was codified in the 1972 constitution, which declared the country a "unitary state" – one in which only the Sinhalese could claim the right to self-determination.

Second were the political failures of opposition parties, which on one hand took the form of an impotent Tamil parliamentary bloc in Colombo – beggars for a slice of the island's pie, who offered only crumbs to their constituents. Their lobbying for equal rights, federalism or autonomy could not stall the increasing scope of national oppression. Their non-violent mass mobilisations were brutally crushed, narrowing the range of possible outlets for Tamil resistance. On the other hand, the large southern Marxist parties failed to take the Tamil national question seriously or, worse, capitulated to or embraced chauvinism. In the 1940s, The Communist Party of Ceylon and the Trotskyist Lanka Sama Samaja Party supported Tamil national rights. But they drifted into the chauvinist camp.

The exploited and impoverished Sinhalese in the south should have been natural allies of the Tamil population. Yet their leaders never mobilised them in solidarity with their oppressed brothers and sisters. Instead, unemployed and landless Sinhalese were roused to religious fervour by demagogic monks and used as settler-battalions in colonisation schemes to alter the demography of Tamil-majority areas. The aim was to reduce Tamil political representation, to take over fertile areas in Tamil country, to undermine the economic position of Tamil fishers and farmers, and to interrupt the contiguity of Tamil homelands, thereby countering the geographic case for a separate state. Further, Sinhalese mobs launched regular anti-Tamil pogroms.

From the 1970s, Tamil radicals could count not one reliable po-

litical ally on the island. So they turned to armed struggle, determined to establish a state – Tamil Eelam – in which they would rule themselves. The violence spiralled as monks, backed by the police and military, mobilised Sinhalese mobs in more orgies of violence. The 1983 Black July binge of murder, rape and plunder stands out, leaving as many as three thousand dead and more than one hundred thousand homeless. "I am not worried about the opinion of the Tamil people", president Jayawardane reportedly said. "Now we cannot think of them, not about their lives or their opinion ... The more you put pressure in the north, the happier the Sinhala people will be here ... Really if I starve the Tamils out, the Sinhala people will be happy."

LTTE training camps expanded rapidly as Tamils fled the capital; a restive and disorganised population now was more open to the argument to take up arms. After almost four decades of political and physical violence, the Tigers, led by Prabhakaran, became the ascendant political force in the north and east. Their guerrillas were hegemonic among the Tamil armed factions and challenged the Sri Lankan military in battle after battle. Perceived traitors were slain; the embryonic rage of the radicalising Tamil youth moulded into one of the most effective insurgencies of modern times.

— — —

Near a small village in the western Vanni, Adampan in Mannar district, female Tiger guerrillas first engaged the Sri Lankan military in 1986. For several years, young women had demanded their right to self-defence against military atrocities and the anti-Tamil pogroms. Trained in the jungles of Tamil Nadu, the combatants at Adampan, fighting alongside their male comrades, ravaged an army search and destroy mission. It was a pivotal moment leading to a significant expansion of women's recruitment as Tiger fury was unleashed in Tamil Eelam. In 1987-90, the Indian Army – misnamed the Indian

Adampan, Mannar

"We were going to suffer anyway, so why not fight?"

Peace Keeping Force – intervened to help the Sri Lankan government quell the liberation movement and to establish its own influence on the island. An estimated twelve thousand Tamils were killed in the ensuing violence. Vetrichelvi recounts the turmoil. "I moved schools eleven times in three years because of the local war. Twice we shifted to India", she says. Vetrichelvi joined the LTTE in 1991. Like Santhia and other across the island, she was in high school at the time. "We joined the LTTE because we wanted to bring the war to an end", she says. "We wanted to get our liberation in a short time. Such a terrible country we lived in. The security forces were terrible to us. We didn't know when they would come, when they would attack. Often, we couldn't sleep. We were going to suffer anyway, so why not fight?"

The LTTE women's wing was controversial. In Tamil society, women's roles are generally fastened to family life. The entrance of women into the guerrilla movement generated both resistance and debate. But, analogous to the situation faced by leaders of industrial economies, some Tiger leaders, Prabhakaran in particular, recognised that expansion required a mobilisation of the whole population. Social barriers were broken as a matter of necessity. "Early Tamil literature is full of episodes which glorify the selfless, sacrificing mothers and wives encouraging bravery and heroism in their sons and husbands", Adele Ann Balasingham, an Australian nurse who played a leading role in the Tigers, wrote in 1993. "But there is a studied silence on women in combat. The Women's Military Unit of Liberation Tigers has changed all that; they have altered the trajectory of Tamil history and introduced a radical new dimension into the history of Tamil women."

Guerrilla life, however, was regimented within a command structure under Prabhakaran's unchallenged authority. There was no Tiger democracy. In the West, Balasingham was criticised for her promotion of a nationalist feminism that reinforced "existing patterns of gender construction". Some of these criticisms were valid. But women former soldiers speak of the confidence gained through the struggle, fighting side by side with their male comrades and winning their respect. They made tangible gains through brute force, rather than by retreating to a non-existent safe space. Under the circumstances, this was no small feat. Vetrichelvi's story embodies the contradictions. Her brother, also a Tiger and concerned for her safety, didn't want Vetrichelvi in the military wing of the organisation. The obliging sister joined the army band as a drummer instead. Two years later, her right arm was blown off below the elbow – a misfire during weapons training in Mullaitivu. She then turned to journalism, undertaking duties in the Tiger's propaganda radio unit, Voice of the Tigers, as an announcer and producer before joining the board of censors for LTTE TV. Though a non-combatant, each role challenged existing sensibilities.

Today, Vetrichelvi is back in the Adampan area, living in the family home next to a vast paddy field. Short, bespectacled and full of cheer, she is a survivor, talking nonchalantly of overcoming life's obstacles as a matter of course, everything an exercise in adaption. The exceptional here is normal. She is famous for penning a trilogy of books: about the Tigers, the final days of the war and life in an internment camp, which was her lot for a year after war's end. Like others, she remains under surveillance; the security forces will be informed of today's visit. Unlike others, these days she doesn't worry. She had numerous fights with them because of her writings. Her profile is now high enough that she is comfortable talking openly about the war. "Santhia was one of my best friends", she says, relating background to Santhia's upbringing before stopping abruptly, determined to prevent clouds of grief from blocking her sunny disposition. Sensing that the emotional storm has passed, she continues. "She was like a mother to the women soldiers." Despite the gains, some stereotypes are hard to shake.

Vetrichelvi

Vidattaltivu, Mannar

EXODUS

Another explosion
Tore away from gravity
Sliced through the cosmos
Light waves ahead of sound waves
Elucidate that brightness to the stars.

In the heat of their last breath
Of those unique souls
Destroying the destructive ship
The ocean heaved once more.

Keep looking sons and daughters
The footprints of freedom sculptors
The true allies of humanity
You will find them here.

Let the interpreters on this globe
Interpret their heart.
Let the researchers on this globe
Research their dedication.

Oh, the waves that kissed them last
When you touch the shores
Whisper in the ears of our people
When freedom is won they will be back.

– Barathy, "Whisper in their ears"

Jaffna

The early monsoon came heavy,

leaving parts of Jaffna peninsula waterlogged. Today, the place is a sultry, taxing fog. West of Point Pedro-Maruthankerny Road, an inland sea overwhelms the flatlands and paddies from which islands of palmyra reach for the clouds. To the east it's sand dunes and scrub. Corrugated and potholed, the road is a 10km-an-hour disaster over which the Vadamarachchi lagoon seems ready to splay to the Bay of Bengal. There is a school here. The Nagar Kovil Maha Vidyalayam hosts a shrine to dead children, victims of an air force attack in September 1995. "There had been bombings the previous day around nearby villages. After lunch, bombs started falling around the village, people started running. Some of the children were hiding under trees outside the school."

Annaludsmy Kandasamy, a former teacher, sits with the principal in a small office recounting the offensive. Children in blue and white uniforms stand to attention. A new generation giggles and grins. But there is no escaping the scars. Ruined homes dot the landscape approaching the village – more markers of the conflict's shifting front. A tamarind trunk – twisted, ghostly – lies near St Joseph Road around the corner from the school.

Kannan, a good student according to Kandasamy, was thirteen when shrapnel severed his lanky frame. His younger brother Aran took shelter with others to avoid the raid. "I don't know what really happened, it all happened in a flash", he says, speaking in Australia, where he now lives. "I was hiding under tamarind trees. Many other children were there – I can't remember how many of us, but there were four trees with a huge canopy." Across from the trees stands the Mylvaganam family home. At the front of the yard is a Besser block wall with an iron gate. "My mum was standing there. She had just returned from the temple. She was crying and calling our names", Aran says. "I ran to the house. That's when a bomb fell. You can hear the bomb coming – the whistling sound. You hear the whistling, but you don't know where it's going to hit. But it hits. Smoke and dust everywhere." The planes left. The dust settled. Now screaming rang out as reality set in. "Kannan had managed to get into the yard. He was inside the gate. But both of his legs were gone – everything below the waist. He was just bleeding, crying for water. At the tamarind trees there were bodies everywhere. One of my friend's insides were hanging from the branches. It was an awful scene."

A week after the Nagar Kovil massacre, the army invaded the peninsula. By the end of October, with infantry approaching, the LTTE evacuated Jaffna. A colossal exodus of half a million people, a human flood amid monsoon rains, moved through choke points across the Uppu Aru lagoon and, later, across the Jaffna lagoon – by boat, across a bridge, by any means – to get to

Tamarind trees, Nagar Kovil

"Kannan had managed to get into the yard. He was inside the gate. But both of his legs were gone – everything below the waist. He was just bleeding, crying for water. At the tamarind trees there were bodies everywhere. One of my friend's insides were hanging from the branches. It was an awful scene."

the shelter of the Vanni, where the Tigers were burrowed before the approaching fury. "It is frightening to walk on the empty streets", S. Edwin Savundra's *War Diary from Jaffna* records. "The cattle and dogs, abandoned by their masters, are in control." Savundra, a philosopher at Saint Francis Xavier's Major Seminary, was one of the few to stay in the town, tending to the infirm and elderly unable to flee. By early December, tens of thousands of mortars had pummelled the city; the military vanquished Tiger rule in the cultural capital of Tamil Eelam. "There is a sense of triumph and victory in [the troops'] faces. 'Your time has gone, now our time has come' is the message that they are giving to the people whom they meet in the captured town of Jaffna", he wrote. "There are many victory banners hung all over the street with various titles … 'Daring, Determined and Done!! This is allways a Sinhalies Country' (note the spelling)."

Exhausted, hungry and demoralised, many returned to their homes under occupation. Others continued to Kilinochchi and its surrounds. The LTTE, vulnerable to a northern offensive, overran a north-eastern army compound in July 1996. Mullaitivu was a garrison town, one of the largest military bases in the country, from which almost the entire Tamil population had fled half a decade before. The force of the Tiger assault stunned the government in Colombo. "Over twelve hundred soldiers were killed in action", Sri Lankan major general Kamal Gunaratne wrote in his 2016 war memoir *Road to Nandikadal*. "The debacle at Mullaitivu went down in the annals of military history as one of the most painful and humiliating defeats ever."

The army launched a counteroffensive in October, taking Kilinochchi and forcing another eastern exodus. The LTTE retook Kilinochchi two years later, but Mullaitivu became the Tigers' nerve centre for the next thirteen years. "We always said publicly that Kilinochchi was the centre of the LTTE. But that was mainly a diversion to keep all the visiting foreign journalists there", a former

Tiger cadre says with a wry smile. "The leadership and command structures were in Mullaitivu. Movement in and out was tightly controlled and monitored." The remains of a Sea Tiger dockyard, along with the experimental vessels tested there, are still accessible north of Mullivaikal. So too a diver training facility – the notice board calls it a "terrorist pool" – now a tourist attraction at the heart of the military's sprawling 68th divisional headquarters in thick jungle near Iranaippalai. Not far away are the remains of Prabhakaran's twelve-metre-deep bunker-compound, ordered destroyed by the government in 2013. Santhia ran a training camp for women fighters in this area. She got about on a motorbike, always smiling. "Before she came to the Black Tigers, she was wounded in battle – one hand was damaged badly", Thulasi, a former comrade who profiled Black Tiger cadres for the LTTE propaganda unit, relates over Skype from Europe. "She wasn't a military trainer, she oversaw the whole camp, documenting its performance and activity and making sure its needs were met."

Government forces retook the southern Vanni by October 1999 after a two-year campaign to clear a land route to Jaffna from the south. It was the largest military operation to that point. Maran (not his real name), a former comrade of Santhia, recounts one mission. An army offensive to the south had killed many women Tigers. The soldiers mutilated their bodies as a warning to the Tamil population not to support the LTTE. Soon after, Tiger commando units in Mullaitivu were instructed to move into enemy territory. "The general mood was that we were on the losing side. We thought we were just on a revenge mission", he says. "There were four or five army artillery camps in the central-eastern Vanni. Seven four-person Black Tiger units, each with a supply team, moved in advance and stationed themselves close to the compounds. Their job was to 'interfere' with Sri Lankan operations."

Commandos from Santhia's camp played a critical role

neutralising the military's Vanni headquarters. After Black Tigers dismantled the enemy's artillery positions, discipline collapsed among the Sinhalese soldiers. It took only five days to reclaim the territory lost over the previous two years as the army retreated in the face of the LTTE onslaught. Santhia, Maran and Thulasi travelled south with a commando team toward another Sri Lankan base in the eastern province. But disaster struck. "In the morning of 5 November, part of the Black Tigers unit was operating in government-controlled territory. Along the way there was a place called Nedunkeni, which had been captured by the LTTE the previous day", Thulasi says. "The Black Tigers unit was resting. We were caught up in a Sri Lankan Air Force raid on the town. Two were killed, including the unit commander … Everyone was panicked and shocked." Maran, who provided explosives support to the commandos, remembers:

"It was early morning and I was making tea. I left to find water. I might have been about three hundred metres away. I saw the plane coming down and I took cover. A bomb hit our position. Santhia was left to take charge. We retreated several kilometres and stayed overnight under tamarind trees. We spent all night talking about the other victories we were hearing about over the radio. We didn't know that there was a broad-ranging offensive. We only knew about our own mission. No-one could believe it happened so quickly, taking back the ground. And we lost only thirty-seven cadres. In the morning, we received news that the brother of one of our team had been killed in another battle. Santhia had to break the news and console her. She had to do it all: food, logistics, communication and consoling. She was an outstanding leader."

The southern Vanni campaign was an early shot in the LTTE's Operation Unceasing Waves III, which aimed to take the vital Elephant Pass linking Jaffna and the Vanni. The Tigers claimed victory in April 2000, the area wrenched from the grip of the occupying army – another disaster for the government in Colombo and the military high command. Black Tiger commandos operated like darts penetrating under the enemy's skin before a barrage of arrows struck at their hearts. But this time, Santhia's poise wavered. "There was an incident which almost broke her", Thulasi says. "A team of Black Tigers were deployed very deep into the army-controlled Jaffna district. Santhia and I received a call telling us they had been ambushed. Two leading commanders were killed and the team collapsed. Her good friend was dead. She seemed broken, crying. I was shocked to see her like that. She had always been so strong and responsible." Santhia, like the others, recovered composure. And the Tamil insurgency paralysed military operations. After two years of negotiations, the Sri Lankan government and the LTTE signed a ceasefire in February 2002. But clouds of war remained on the horizon. The storm was approaching.

Shrine to dead children, Nagar Kovil Maha Vidyalayam

Your hands would stretch to stop us speeding.
"Can we come too brother?" you would say.
We would speed without words.

If we had forgotten to dim the lights
You would scold in the gendered tone.
A sad smile would come over us.

Oh brothers, we are your sisters.
We fired artilleries non-stop
From stationary launchers.
Then we drove moving launchers
Chasing the escaping enemies.
How then do you decide that
All who drive at night are males?
Throw away your foolish assumptions
And observe the coming changes.

Tomorrow your big sister may drive a HiAce van.
Your little sister may pilot a plane.
Your niece may become the naval commander.
Your daughter may drive the heavy vehicles
To renovate the Tamil Eelam roads.
Hope you would live to see your granddaughter
Roll along this struggling world with one hand.

– Nila, "You – Night – Us"

Tamil Tigers, Jaffna, early 1990s

POWER

Peace talks were met with relief

across the island, but not by everyone. Buddhist clerics, having initially supported the ceasefire, initiated a national mobilisation for holy war when the government appeared to contemplate a federal solution to the Tamil national question. "With protest marches, sit-in strikes and press releases [they] mobilised the population", Weiberg-Salzmann writes. "For the first time in the history of Sri Lanka, the prelates of all three sects jointly released a common statement on the state of the nation. [They] spoke out for a ban on the LTTE, against the union of the northern and eastern provinces, against the retreat of the security forces from the north, for the preservation of the state, against a federal system, and against a transitional government under the LTTE in the north." The army too was unnerved. After more than half a decade ruling Jaffna, it now had to contend with a population growing assertive in the knowledge that its oppressors were restricted in their ability to wage violence – both by the terms of the ceasefire and by the growth of the Tiger apparatus. General Gunaratne lamented the "insults, humiliation and ridicule" endured by forty thousand security personnel occupying the peninsula when he was a brigade commander leading the Sri Lankan occupation of Jaffna:

"Segments of society in the north and east, which had respected and feared us during the war, started to look at us with disrespect and contempt … Hordes of LTTE who entered the areas under government control were highly successful in brainwashing the youth with their anti-government, anti-Sinhalese and anti-army rhetoric … The hundreds of jobless youth who used to loiter around at junctions were rejuvenated by the LTTE presence. Three wheeler drivers were acting with a newfound sense of authority and drove around as if they owned the roads. Driving in the middle of the road, they blocked army vehicles from overtaking, ignoring the blaring horns. Youth on motorcycles would ride around perniciously, overtaking army vehicles whilst loudly spewing filth at us. The army drivers underwent severe hardship and even the smallest of accidents turned into chaos, abuse, pelting of stones and death threats. The junctions were controlled by the wheeler drivers who were power unto themselves. Soldiers who ventured into towns to purchase something were abused. Some would purposely bang against these soldiers and turn around and shout in filth … Such attitude and anger was instigated by the LTTE, who gave youth the strength to defy authority or even a symbol of authority."

For all the particularities of the Tamil Eelam national struggle, it shares something with every movement for liberation: there always emerges a Gunaratne – some proud authority unable to comprehend the hatred of the people whose everyday deference is interpreted as a sincere display, rather than a performance later cursed in private. Tiger cadres were dedicated, talented and hardworking, but their skills were limited to more mundane and practical arts than "brainwashing". Three wheeler drivers were restive from years of military occupation. All they needed to own the roads was confidence, and the knowledge that they would be supported in their actions. While the brigade commander licked the psychological wounds inflicted by youths displaying a lack of respect for men in uniform, the Tiger de facto state took firmer form in the Vanni, consolidating the power and authority of the LTTE. A nascent apparatus had developed after the withdrawal of Indian troops in 1990, when the Tigers took Jaffna – the first time that the organisation gained control of and took responsibility for the administration of a significant civilian population. With the town's reoccupation by the Sri Lankan military in 1995, the influx of refugees to the Vanni strained existing infrastructure. But it opened the space for a social experiment.

"Basic goods such as Panadol, sugar, soap and sanitary products all were banned", says Maran. "We never saw petrol; however, kerosene was smuggled from India by boat. But we built an economy that could maintain itself despite this." Much of the Tiger apparatus was reconfigured toward service provision – a shadow administration supplementing the meagre services provided by the existing government bureaucracy. (If Colombo had abandoned the administrative apparatus in LTTE-controlled territory, it would have been viewed by all as a concession to Tamil demands for self-rule. So it kept alive a skeleton bureaucracy.) For example, the government continued to fund the education system in the north, but it was under-resourced. The Tamil Eelam Educational Development Council, led by Catholic priest Francis Joseph, created a teacher program, paid for by the LTTE, that trained young educators. With the cessation of hostilities, the Tiger state grew more expansive and sophisticated as trade resumed, as revenues rose and as a political space opened with the easing of the security situation. "This was a very hopeful period for Tamils across the island and in Tamil Eelam as well as the diaspora", Maran says. The de facto state included a police force and judicial system, education and health institutions, and childcare, banking and land management divisions among others.

Former cadres and civilians talk with pride of three areas of Tiger rule: efforts to eliminate the caste system, women's social gains and the imposition of order. Each area harboured its own contradictions born of the limitations of war, of the society in which the experiments were undertaken and of the LTTE's strategic approach to national liberation. The Tigers made huge inroads eliminating caste divisions and prejudices within their own ranks: lower caste Tamils were heavily represented among cadres and the leadership; their sacrifices as soldiers of the people were venerated. Within the apparatus of the de facto state, there were also gains. N. Malathy, who worked in several human rights and welfare institutions in the Vanni from 2005 to 2009, but who was not a member of the Tigers, recounts in her memoir, *A fleeting moment in my country*:

"South Asian thought patterns, even today, are ridden with caste categorisation. Widespread egalitarian thought is foreign to the region ... The ideologies of the LTTE, which urged the downtrodden to take an active role in the liberation struggle, had challenged this mode of thought. In Vanni, at least within the wider LTTE community, this had created a social context where the old caste- and class-based thought processes had been challenged. This new way of conceptualising society brought a particular calibre of people into leadership roles in the social work organisations. Many of these leaders came from the oppressed communities of the earlier social formation ... They therefore carried [these sensibilities] into their social work arena, creating a social cohesion that had rarely been seen previously. It was these social processes that had created the unique

culture observable in most social work organisations operating in LTTE-administered areas."

Among the broader Tamil population too there were steps forward. One example was hairdressers, a lower caste. Upper caste people previously did not go to salons; they believed themselves dirtied by association. Instead, barbers would come to their homes. The hairdressers' association, supported by the LTTE, eliminated this practice. This might seem trivial, but the caste system was full of practices that sapped the dignity of lower caste people. The challenges of the military siege, combined with demands for social cohesion, created mixed results. For example, a man in the north from the fisher caste explains that Tigers sometimes turned a blind eye to existing caste practices because of the conflict arising from the organisation's dual goals of furthering social equality and maintaining national unity. The LTTE was in control, but some wealthier and upper caste Tamils accepted Tiger power only pragmatically, rather than enthusiastically. Unity of all classes and castes therefore resulted in concessions to avoid strife on all fronts.

The gains of, and contradictions within, the struggle for equality of the sexes have been noted. It is worth quoting Malathy again for a picture of life on the ground under the de facto state. She stands out as one of the few observers writing in the English language combining sympathy for, and criticism of, LTTE rule:

"Militarism permitted many liberating characteristics for women. The training improved their demeanour that was otherwise conditioned by a culture that demanded a strictly subordinate role. Participation in battles raised their status to that of the LTTE men in the eyes of the general population. It gave them the freedom to act in the public space in ways that were clearly different from the rest of the women. This … had a flow on effect for the civilian women too. There were many non-military areas in which Vanni society exhibited greater pro-women character than the wider Tamil society … Just observing the number of women on the streets during peak hours dressed for work, it was obvious that a greater percentage of women in Vanni went to work outside the home. There were also more women in civilian clothes riding motorbikes on Vanni roads compared to the rest of the island. Women, both LTTE members as well as civilians, occupied the public space in large numbers. They were very visible on the roads and in the LTTE institutions. This gave Vanni a uniquely pro-woman character, which was absent elsewhere on the island …

"Yet, visually, the most obvious sign of oppressive habits among civilian women in Vanni was also the practice of wearing the saree [a traditional dress designed for modesty and which restricts the sort of activities a wearer can easily perform] by even those employed in LTTE civilian institutions. Thousands of civilian women worked in such institutions, and they were all compelled to wear the saree in a uniform style determined by the LTTE institution. The contrast was striking for anyone who cared to observe it. It was shocking to see the saree being made compulsory for civilian women working in LTTE institutions, when LTTE women wore trousers and shirts as their uniform. Many young women have told me that they resisted applying for jobs in LTTE institutions because of the compulsion to wear the saree. Almost all women resisted this practice. LTTE women were vocal about their resistance and they were never subjected to it. Civilian women on the other hand were subjected to this rule … These different tensions acting on the issue of female attire accurately captured the status of women's issues in general in Vanni."

In Western countries, law and order is the terrain of the political right because the police and courts disproportionately target poor and oppressed groups and ensure economic and political stability for the ruling class. But for an oppressed society under siege and engaged in resistance, disorder and uncertainty are diabolical enemies. They foster suspicion and

sap solidarity's resolve, fracturing the unity of purpose without which no struggle for liberation can succeed. People in Jaffna consistently raise two benefits of LTTE law and order: vengeance against gendered violence, which created a space for women to walk alone in the evening and at night without harassment, and crackdowns on anti-social behaviour, which led to the absence of drugs and drunks on the street. Both were considered vital for enabling popular participation in the struggle, for generating trust in Tiger rule and for preventing the growth of a class of addicts and felons who might be bribed or blackmailed by agents of the Sri Lankan government.

— — —

While the Tamils had been forced by events to take up arms, limitations in the LTTE's approach became evident. Tiger ascendency among the factions in the 1980s at times involved the eradication of competitors. They were not alone in dishing out violence; most factions engaged in, to put it diplomatically, un-savoury practices. The pressures for this are obvious. Those taking the road of armed struggle are bound to be more adept at, and prone to, using physical force to resolve differences. It is one of the great weaknesses of armed struggle as a strategy, rather than a sometime tactic, that it results in authoritarianism. Anecdotally, this was the case under Tiger rule, other political forces complaining of intimidation at the hands of LTTE cadres.

State-building practicalities also highlighted contradictions in the organisation's nationalist project. Human flourishing is impossible under conditions of national oppression. Oppressed nations therefore have the right to self-determination, including the right to secession. But the creation of a new state within the world imperialist system will always result in new divisions between rulers and ruled, or the solidification and codification of existing divisions that may tem-porarily be papered over during the struggle for emancipation. As

Malathy notes, the Tiger de facto state expressed these emerging tensions as the movement mor-phed from armed struggle to administrative rule:

"Though only a very small percentage of those living in Vanni at this time were bona fide LTTE members ... the majority of working people in Vanni had a close relative from this pool. This factor strongly coloured the social space in Vanni at this time and gave the entire society an LTTE flavour. LTTE institutions were also the major employer, and as a result civilians were further drawn into the LTTE ambit. The large number of LTTE families with children now living in the wider community also brought in another layer of interconnected-ness. This growing interconnect-edness was constantly negated by some of the activities of the LTTE. Foremost among these activities was the everpresent recruitment drive of the LTTE. During this period, the bureaucratic lethargy in some LTTE institutions also came under constant criticism ... I repeatedly heard people saying that the LTTE was increasing its distance from the people."

Conscription embodied this. As the peace process faltered, military considerations again came to the fore. But Tiger recruitment drives fell short and the leadership demanded of each family one recruit to its armed wing. This created much debate – and consternation – within the general population and among Tiger cadres.

— — —

The ceasefire and peace talks resulted from Tiger strength forcing Colombo politicians to the negotiating table when a military solution appeared distant. But after several years, the balance of power shifted. An influx of foreign NGOs and the imposition of international benchmarks for peace weighed on the LTTE. Nowhere was the pressure greater than on the issue of child soldiers. The Tigers were born of a youth radicalisation that aimed for liberation from oppression and for a movement that bypassed the "grown-up" politicians who failed to negotiate a settlement with in-

creasingly ethno-supremacist Sri Lankan governments. Talking with ex-LTTE military cadre in Tamil Eelam, most joined the struggle as adolescents and many, particularly the young women, had to fight for their right to self-defence to be recognised. But the United Nations Optional Protocol on the involvement of children in armed conflict, which came into force as the peace process began, created dual standards. Until this time, the Convention on the Rights of the Child held that governments "should not allow children under fifteen to join the army". However, while the new protocol banned governments from compulsorily recruiting people under eighteen, it said that armed groups not recognised as state forces should not under any circumstances use them in hostilities. This weaponised the rights of the child against the targets of genocide; the international community's exhortation to think of the children was an instruction to Tamil youth to lie down and die.

The UN knew full well that warfare between the Sri Lankan Army and the Liberation Tigers was asymmetric. The former had far greater conventional military strength. Despite their advances, the Tigers still relied on ambush, stealth and political conviction. They also employed suicide bombings, a modern hallmark of relative military weakness. This weakness was compounded by the NGOs' and the United Nations' narrow focus on child soldiers to the detriment of other human rights. "*A fleeting moment* was written immediately after I got out of the internment camp and thus based solely on what I observed during those years in Vanni under the ceasefire agreement and later as it broke down", Malathy says via email from her home in New Zealand. "During those years I observed the blatant bias of NGOs and the UN agencies." The liberation movement was under pressure from the UN and NGOs to adopt "norms" of warfare between states, which further weakened the Tigers' fighting position.

"The struggle for a Tamil homeland was not wanting in sustained popular support, heroism and courage, discipline or sacrifices",

Radha D'Souza, a writer and critic based at the University of Westminster, argues. "The struggle got mired in the peace process. The peace process was the beginning of the end of the Tamil struggle for a homeland. The peace process softened up the resistance of a war weary nation. It engaged with the resistance on social standards, including human rights, demanding from it the same universal standards as a state with full membership of the UN; but it did so without recognising the demand for statehood. In other words, it was a demand to live up to high ethical standards without the institutional preconditions for it ... The demand for international social and cultural standards from the LTTE without statehood enabled the peacemakers and international media to discredit the claims of the entire Tamil nation ... [and put] organised Tamil resistance on hold. After the softening up was achieved the peacemakers packed up and left, leaving the ground open for a full scale military operation by the Sri Lankan state."

"The demand for international social and cultural standards from the LTTE without statehood enabled the peacemakers and international media to discredit the claims of the entire Tamil nation."

The tall buildings of UN
Stands strong and high
On the strength of human bones
Its colourful flags flutter – like
Countless lives it swallowed

You talk betterment of life
But look down under the red carpet
Human bodies wriggle like worms
Portends your blinded eyes to open

Hen protects its young
But you protect the vultures
Bloated with lives of the poor
The vulture's belly peaks out
Unable to hide under your wings

Like an ostrich hiding its head
You hide behind "world peace"
Your face is not visible
But your body is so naked.

You claim the right to declare
The rights of all humans
Our people, our rights, we declare
When our strength grows – with
Our skill and dedication
You will come to set things "right"
We will then teach you
Our experience of freedom.

– Barathy, "Oh the UN ..."

THE
BEACH

Mullivaikal

58

Mullivaikal

The Mullivaikal sky today is grey.

Clouds stretch to the horizon, dulling the east coast's choppy waters. Fishing boats on the sand impress on visitors an image of un-interrupted traditional village life. But permanent sentries from the sprawling naval base to the south are reminders that something isn't right. Not too far from the beach, where wildflowers blossom and the scrub begins, terror is etched into the earth. Remnants of bunkers dug in desperation scar the ground. Mangled pieces of iron and severed palm trunks lie among what's left of people's belongings. Shoes, tangled saree scraps and other discarded items remain almost a decade after their owners departed. Each is a marker of one of history's great horrors.

"I will never forget that day", one survivor recounts. "They buried us alive." Many houses here have been rebuilt, but there is an eerie lack of life. Aside from the sea breeze, everything is still. On this tiny thread of desolation between the ocean and Nandikadal lagoon, the dry earth blew shrapnel amid a monsoon of mortars. More than one hundred thousand were hemmed in, their senses pounded and their bodies strafed. There was no shelter. No way out. "Very terrible things happened here", a local relates. "We were herded like cattle to this place. Someone had a hoe; we used it and our hands to dig. Our clothes, sarees, we filled them with sand to make walls on the bunkers … We didn't have enough time to bury the dead. Every day we counted them: one hundred, one hundred and fifty … In the last days, thousands. The army used phosphorus. I can still remember the smell."

Sri Lankan military commanders called this place a "no fire zone" – a safe space in which to cover. Then they turned it into a mass grave, deliberately shelling civilians and bombing the makeshift medical facilities in a premeditated extermination. By mid-May 2009, tens of thousands of bodies littered Mullivaikal and the area to its north-west. "The battle has reached its bitter end", conceded the LTTE. "We have decided to silence our guns." The Tigers were annihilated. But there was a final humiliation: on the last day of the war, former comrades emerged wearing Sri Lankan Army uniforms. "We were shocked. They were double agents", Vetrichelvi says.

The army said that surviving LTTE members would be arrested and interned. Most were. But as Callum Macrae's documentary film *No Fire Zone* later uncovered, many were tortured, mutilated and summarily executed. Images filmed by government soldiers as war trophies show naked, desecrated bodies of women Tigers. "I would like to fuck it again", a soldier says, surveying one of the corpses on the ground. Survivors were marched south and transported to prison camps. One Tamil Catholic pastor recounted the

"I will never forget that day. They buried us alive."

"We were herded like cattle to this place."

"The army used phosphorus. I can still remember the smell."

situation to Jon Lee Anderson, a staff writer at the *New Yorker*: "We were walking out through fire and past dead people, and the soldiers were laughing at us and saying, 'We have killed all your leaders. Now you are our slave'".

— — —

In the photo, Karuna Amman wears a smart, purple-striped French-cuff shirt tucked into a pair of dress pants. Now minister for national integration in the Sri Lankan government, he clearly has enriched himself. It is 18 May 2009 and the former eastern commander of the LTTE is surrounded by military officers. The war is over. He grins, surveying Velupillai Prabhakaran's lifeless body. A handkerchief rests over the Tiger leader's forehead, covering the bullet wound marking his execution. Karuna is a rat who helped slay the Tigers. Exactly why he broke ranks is contested, but in 2004 the colonel lead a rebellion against the northern command. He managed to take only several dozen cadres with

him, so the LTTE rapidly took back control of the east. But the split was debilitating: thousands were lost to demoralisation. In a supreme act of betrayal, Karuna provided intelligence to the Sri Lankan military and later formed a paramilitary organisation that worked with the army to destroy the LTTE's eastern apparatus. All Tiger-controlled areas from Ampara through Trincomalee and beyond were conquered by mid-2007. There was far more to it than Karuna's defection, however. Several other factors contributed to the decimation of one of the most feared insurgencies in modern history.

First, Mahinda Rajapaksa, a hardline Sinhalese chauvinist, won the country's presidential election in November 2005. Immediately, the change in government was felt through a rise in disappearances and extrajudicial killings in areas controlled by the Sri Lankan Army. The new president vowed to wipe out the Tigers, rejecting a political settlement to safeguard the national rights of Tamils. He appointed his army-veteran brother, Gotabaya, as secretary of defence and a fellow hardliner, Sarath Fonseka, as army commander. They transformed the military as the government increased the defence budget by 40 percent. "Earlier we would recruit approximately three thousand [soldiers] per year, but now we are achieving targets of three thousand per month. Immediately after we took [the east], we managed to recruit six thousand in a single month", Fonseka told *Business Today*'s Malinda Seneviratne in December 2008. "The strength of the army when I took over was one hundred and sixteen thousand. Today it stands at one hundred and seventy thousand … I created fifty new battalions."

Second, the Buddhist sangha continued to assert itself. The monks founded the National Sinhala Heritage Party, which allowed only clerics to run as candidates for parliament. "According to their party manifesto, Sri Lanka was 'a-dharma' (unjust) and 'a-rajika' (headless); therefore religious actors must

take over leadership of the state … The political system was to be ritually purified with the help of Buddhism", Weiberg-Salzmann notes. "While the monks promised to stand up for equal rights for all the country's religions and ethnicities, they still claimed supremacy for the Sinhalese: 'There is only one nation in this country, viz. the Sinhalese. The right to self-determination is only vested in them' … The monks spoke out for a 'Sinhala Nation', a 'Dhamma Kingdom' – a state built upon Buddhist principle 'to save the future of our race and religion'."

Third, the Tigers' increasing strength highlighted the limits of their military strategy. The more the guerrillas came to approximate a conventional army, the more their relative weakness was exposed as they engaged on their opponent's terms. The LTTE was already at a disadvantage in terms of hardware. The pool from which it could recruit soldiers was also smaller than that of the Sri Lankan armed forces, the Tamil population being little more than ten percent of the island. The loss of cadres in the east and the realisation that the enemy was building its fighting resources led to the controversial Tiger conscription program – but it was impossible to match the recruitment drive of the army. And it was difficult to build an effective resistance when enlistment depended on compulsion rather than conviction. As general Gunaratne noted, conscription was an acknowledgement that the LTTE now had to focus on quantity rather than quality in building its forces. Its capacity was thus degraded even as its numbers increased.

These three factors were not decisive, though. The national liberation movement was powerful; it likely would have withstood everything the Sri Lankan government threw at it. But the international balance of forces turned against the Tigers, ultimately sealing their fate. India, the key regional power with an interest in the island, had directly intervened once, only to be beaten back by the guerrillas. After that, and after the collapse of the Soviet Union, it built new alliances. "As a junior

Monument to the dead, Mullivaikal

partner, [it] formed a strategic alliance with the US, and then on, increasingly subordinated its strategic policy approach towards Sri Lanka under the US war paradigm, becoming complicit in the genocidal process against the Tamil people", noted the 2013 final report of the Permanent Peoples' Tribunal on Sri Lanka.[1]

The Tigers were banned in India and the US in the 1990s. Britain, Canada and the European Union followed in the twenty-first century. In 2005-06 a major international crackdown crippled the Tigers' fundraising efforts in diaspora heartlands. There was proactive support for Rajapaksa's regime, which, despite its rearmament program, did not have the capacity on its own to conquer the north-east. Peter Layton, writing in the Asia-Pacific magazine *Diplomat* noted US assistance in "disrupting LTTE offshore military equipment procurement, sharing intelligence, providing a Coast Guard vessel, and supplying an important national naval command and control system". This was key: Sea Tiger losses mounted, depriving ground forces of supplies. The LTTE had eleven cargo ships that transported military equipment from around the world. All of them were destroyed with intelligence support from India and the United States, the last in 2007.

Support also came from states at odds with the West. Aid worth billions of dollars was offered by China, Russia, Iran, Libya and Pakistan. Big finance weighed in as well. With Colombo debt-loading to annihilate the liberation movement, the global financial crisis gave added urgency to repayments. Creditors knew that the Sri Lankan government's fiscal situation was unsustainable and wanted the war over quickly. Burns Strider, an adviser to Hillary Clinton, emailed the then US secretary of state in 2009: "This is about Sri Lankan Govt and the Tigers … I have a good source … [T]he people on the ground both with World Bank and IMF believe the Tigers need to be completely defeated and any collateral damage inflicted on private people by [Sri Lankan] govt in process is ok".

Santhia and Kumaran had a "love marriage" that transcended caste and defied social norms. Their relationship was built on solidarity, struggle and the mutual understanding of two people devoted to a common cause. To an outsider, love marriage is at first glance a peculiar designation. But including the word "love" signifies a wedlock at odds with Tamil tradition, which usually involves an arrangement by families, rather than the two people intimately involved, and which requires a dowry of cash, goods and/or property to the groom's family. The Tigers resolved to abolish the dowry system, opening the way for greater freedoms for individuals, particularly women, to enter relationships on their own terms. Sometime after the peace process began, Santhia settled in Kilinochchi to start a family with Kumaran, their bond an exemplar of the higher union – free association – to which the LTTE aspired for the Tamil nation.

It proves difficult to glean from friends and former comrades much information about Santhia the individual and her personal life. They talk about her sense of duty, and her demeanour and leadership qualities within the organisation. A friend becomes irritated by repeated inquiries about the poets and writers Santhia read, and what hobbies she had. Why would someone travel so far for such a banal inquisition? After some time trying to gain insights about Santhia's own poetry, the answer is curt, the friend's deadpan expression a demand for the line of questioning to end: "She wrote about the soldiers' feelings: what they are feeling about Eelam and what they are feeling about the LTTE and our leader".

The point, which I took too long to acknowledge, is that the personal was subsumed under the struggle for national liberation. Individual desires never disappeared of course. Ex-cadres fondly recall the campfire discussions during which they got to know one another, and speak of the comradeship formed in the Vanni jungles. But the LTTE

"The knife is at our throat."

could not tolerate individualism or harbour dilettantes. Nowhere is this clearer than when sitting with Vetrichelvi, who grins recounting the struggle, half an arm missing and many of her friends dead. There is not an ounce of self-pity here. The moment emotions threaten to get the better of her is one of deep embarrassment – a regrettable breach of discipline on the part of a cadre who fought too long to let her guard lapse.

Regardless of one's evaluation of the Tigers – of their politics, of their strategy or of the tactics they sometimes employed – there is something uplifting here: a collective for whom the cause of everyone's liberation was superior to the advance of any individual's interest. The seriousness with which this was taken is illustrated by the ceremony after completing basic training: every graduate presented with a necklace bearing not a jewel, but a cyanide capsule to be swallowed in the event of capture. The struggle portended freedom, but death hung over the hearts of those most committed to the cause.

—— —— ——

A year after the fall of the east, Mannar was taken in August 2008. The noose was tightening. In September, the government ordered all UN expatriate staff out of LTTE-controlled territory. "There was this large crowd of people outside [of the UN compound in Kilinochchi] and they were really pleading with us – as the UN, as the international community – please don't leave", Benjamin Dix, a former UN staffer, recalls in *No Fire Zone*. "I remember driving out of there, just full of shame and guilt and confusion of this organisation that I worked for and what it apparently stood for. And we drove out … What we'd actually done was complete abandonment of our duty of protection of civilians in a conflict situation." The Sri Lankan government told the world of its "humanitarian" operation to "rescue civilians" from the clutches of "terrorists". But those on the ground knew better what was coming. In the crowd, an elderly man pleads with the cameraman: "We are begging you to stay … If we allow you to leave, the truth is that everyone here will die. The knife is at our throat".

Four months later, Kilinochchi fell. Santhia joined yet another exodus. Hundreds of thousands of Tamils fled east as Sri Lankan troops encircled and pushed deep into the Vanni. "The LTTE's political structures and institutions … were gradually closed down and abandoned as the insurgents lost territory", Joanne Richards notes in a 2014 Centre on Conflict, Development and Peacebuilding working paper. "On 21 January 2009 the Sri Lankan government unilaterally declared a 'No Fire Zone' within an area of LTTE-held territory in Vanni … While the government claimed that the security forces were 'fully committed' to providing 'maximum safety for civilians', the army subjected the no fire zone to sustained heavy bombardment … As the frontlines moved further east, the government abrogated the first no fire zone and, on 12 February 2009, created a second, smaller no fire zone on a narrow strip of land on the east coast north of Mullaitivu.

This action marked the beginning of a pattern in which the government declared ever smaller no fire zones and then continued on the offensive, pushing the LTTE's frontlines back."

Tiger attempts to broker a new ceasefire fell on deaf ears in Colombo. Over the next three months, their cadres and leadership suffered heavy losses. The organisation became virtually headless, commando units fighting again as guerrillas but surrounded and without coordination or support. Eventually, Prabhakaran realised the battle was lost and sent word that LTTE cadres could try to escape. Many fought on, including most of the senior leadership, who were systematically wiped out. Santhia was somewhere around here, but no-one can say when or how she got out after the fall of Kilinochchi. The haze of battle and passing time result in imprecise testimonies. "After Kilinochchi, no-one had a set base", Maran says. "Santhia was closer to the leadership, so was probably stationed near Prabhakaran. But she was not on bodyguard duties at that time because she had an infant with her." (The Imran Pandian unit was responsible for the Tiger leader's security). Whatever happened, Santhia survived. Within a year, she fled with her baby boy to India. She never saw her husband again.

--- --- ---

We have been stopped by the military for questioning only once. They seem more relaxed now that eight and a half years have passed since conquering the north. But among many Tamils, the tension is palpable. At a small farmhouse in the Vanni, a woman breaks down and pleads for us to leave. We are talking with her brother, who wants to explain more of what happened in Mullivaikal and of the years leading to the bitter end. But the two are all that is left of their family and the thought of more trouble from the government is over-whelming. He relents in the face of his sister's obvious distress. They are not the only ones who hesitate. Others also refuse to speak – those who have lost so much that all they

can do is try to piece together their lives and not draw undue attention from state security. The siblings know the truth in all its awful detail. Many like them will spare even their children the retelling and take to their graves the horrors they witnessed, hoping the next generation avoids such a terrible fate. It is understandable – no-one is left to protect them.

Half an hour's drive away, in Mullaitivu town, a local man climbs quickly and with discretion into our van. The Criminal Inves-tigation Department, notorious for kidnapping and disappearing suspected former LTTE members and activists committed to Tamil liberation, maintains a presence here. Siva (not his real name) directs the driver to a nearby field at Vadduvakal, a couple of kilometres south from the killing fields of Mullivaikal. Here they were marched, he says, into a preliminary displacement camp, before being sent inland to the larger prison camps. In these places, the suffering continued. Rapes. Murders. Appalling sani-tation. Disappearances of those suspected of having links to the Tigers. (Up to thirteen thousand were arrested and detained in separate "rehabilitation" camps.) While Tamils were confined, the military takeover of Tamil Eelam began.

"We had to leave [the dead] and keep moving", Siva says. "My brother lost his right leg; I had to carry him. He was a member of the LTTE … Some soldiers attempted to shoot us. Others helped to carry the injured to the camps and treated us well. All type of [soldiers] were there – the genuine people and …" – he trails off, but his eyes say everything of what was to come next. North of the causeway bridge under which Nandikadal meets the Bay of Bengal, Siva points to the place where Karuna and the military top brass showed off Prabhakaran's body. Pulling out a mobile phone, he brings up pictures taken nearby four years later: parts of another skeleton still scattered at the lagoon's edge. As the fog lifts on this and other human remains, it is clear that not even the dead were laid to rest at war's end.

Site of first internment, Vadduvakal

Midnight ...
Vultures surrounded the village.
Dozing villagers sacrificed to
demon.
My eyes blinded in anger.
A silent war within me.
Have I not been called a terrorist?
Do I not have Tamil Eelam blood?
I joined the list of the disappeared.
My name in hand-cuff
Together with our departed kin
I will wait for the freedom.

– Samarvili, "I will wait ..."

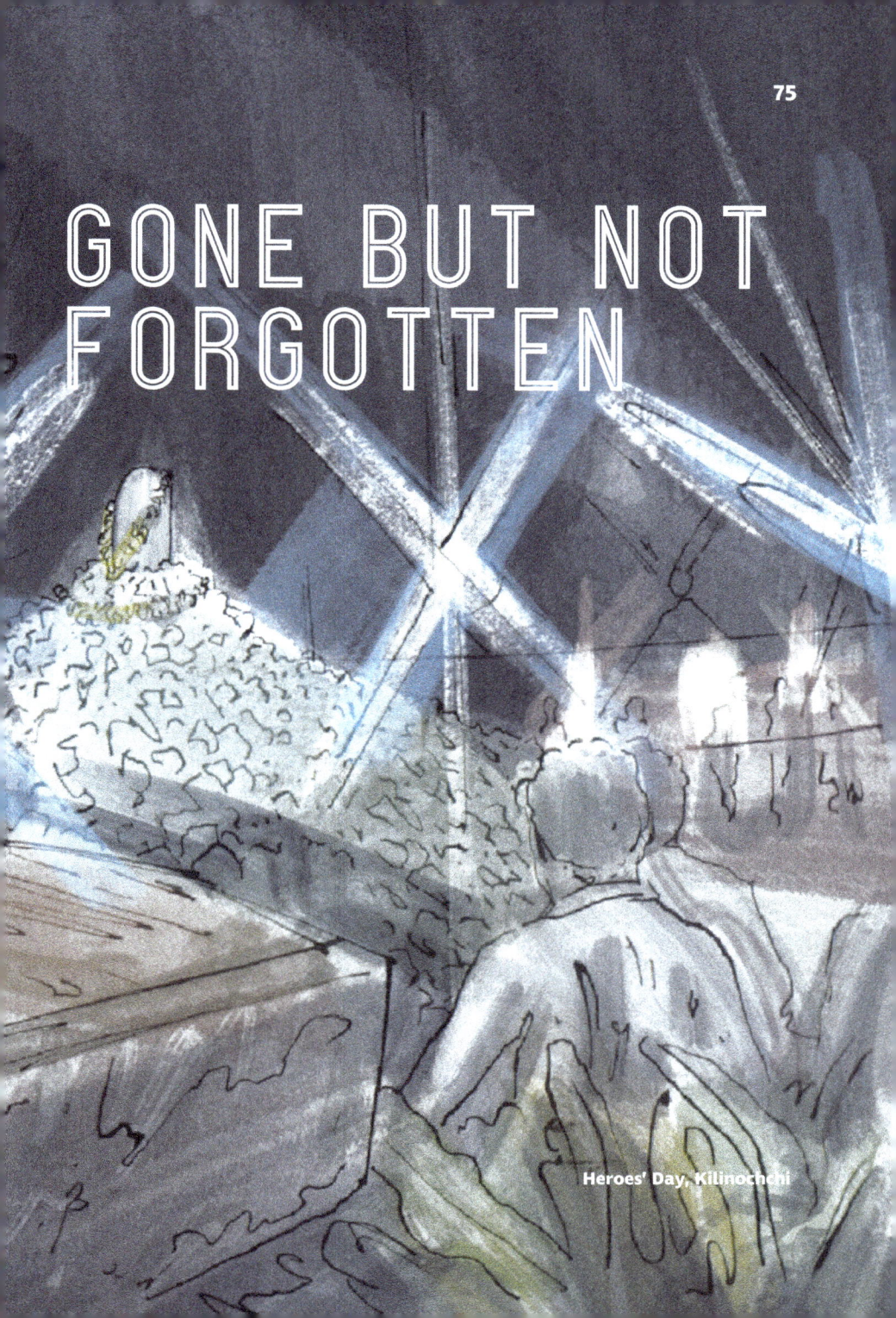

GONE BUT NOT FORGOTTEN

Heroes' Day, Kilinochchi

The boy is beaming.

"My name is Theelipan!"[2] He wants to practise English with his new friend. His sister, grinning, stands nearby, arms straight down her front, hands reverse interlocked and weaving as her torso coils this way and that, the left knee then the right bending – those involuntary movements of a child excited by a visitor. Mother asks that their names be withheld, as the eldest of the three brings biscuits and creamy soda. She is ex-LTTE military wing. Her husband is abroad, a political refugee enduring like the rest. They have been separated for five years. A familiar story. Twice in the last month, the security forces have visited, she says. Within their ranks is a culture of impunity aiding reprisals, torture and disappearances. Even the children are harassed occasionally in this small Mannar district village.

The advances made by women Tigers during the revolutionary war have been noted because social progress can be measured by the breakdown of division and oppression. Women's every step forward was a mirror, then, to the broader reconfiguration of life – everyone stood to gain from the advance of women and lower caste Tamils because all relationships would be enriched as people saw in each other a vision of themselves, rather than simply another to use or remain distant from. The glimpses of equality, forged in struggle, portended a new world. While they remained glimpses, they nevertheless were real. Now, with the destruction of the LTTE de facto state, caste discrimination has made a resurgence, the status of women has declined and there are signs of social breakdown. "The mindset of the LTTE women has changed. Before 2009, there was confidence. Now there is no meaning in death and no meaning in life", Vetrichelvi says, sipping tea in her family's house not far from here. "Many are confined to their homes. Those with skills gained in the LTTE often feel unable to put

Heroes' Day, Vanni

Heroes' Day, Vanni

them to use in postwar society – to do so would bring the scrutiny of the security forces. Only former Tigers are likely to have the skills these women possess."

Many also carry the stigma of defeat. As soldiers, the women had to become something other than what traditional society expected. Now, finding a place in the conservative civilian world around them can be a challenge. "When I was in the movement, whenever I walk into the village in uniform with a rifle I could see the respect people had for me, from the way they looked at me", former Tiger S. Thamilini wrote in her memoir *In the shadow of a sharp edged sword.* "People regarded me as a person who went to war on behalf of them and treated me as their own child … Now I am worthless … Once as female combatants we dreamed of bending the sky like a bow. Now all our dreams have vanished, we have fallen flat on the ground of reality … We dreamed that freeing ourselves from the constraints of home, carrying a rifle, would change our society. What really happened was we female combat-

ants were able to win battles at the warfront, but we were unable to change the ideas of womanhood in our society. The liberation of women of the Tamil community took a leap forward with images of females taking up arms, but sadly this ended with the defeat of the armed struggle."

In Mullaitivu, on the other side of the island, the struggle against the state has resumed under difficult circumstances. "The unity of the people has been broken by many government groups. That has weakened us", a prominent campaigner for the disappeared explains through the translator. "The Criminal Investigation Department has visited my home many times. Since 2010 they come here each and every month and take photographs. Of my daughter as well. My husband was handed over to government forces. We asked for a long time where he was. Finally, in 2012, they sent me a death certificate and one hundred and twenty thousand rupees [about one thousand Australian dollars] – that's all. I sent back the money and the death certificate. I don't want it. It didn't include the reason for his death. Many people in poverty have accepted compensations and certificates because of death threats to their children … Others have been bribed with chickens or cows so that they can make a living. This is one way they try to break the relationship, the bond, among the Tamil people. We started a campaign to ask questions of the government. But as more people have accepted these certificates, our protests have gotten smaller. It has been harder."

There are tens of thousands of "missing" people. This woman's husband was a non-military member of the LTTE, an engineer. They had been in Mullivaikal before being interned. He fell ill and was transferred to Vavunia hospital. Then he disappeared. The military told her they were undertaking additional inquiries and had taken him to Colombo. "You can read about our conclusions in the newspapers", they said. She was pregnant at the time and last saw him on 23 June 2009. Her daughter has never seen her father, but on the wall is a family picture of the three – digitally altered to bring them together in a print portrait. Amid the loss, a determined minority is organising again across the north and the east. Opposite a building occupied by the security forces on one of the main streets of town is a tarpaulin marquee. The women here – mothers, wives – have been in permanent protest for months, demanding to know what happened to their husbands and sons. In Kilinochchi, there's another makeshift structure on the side of the road not far from an army base in the centre of town. They too are refusing to disband until the government tells them the truth about what happened to their loved ones, pictures of whom hang around the interior. The man who has been driving us around the north for the last week points to one – it's his brother. Everyone has been touched by the violence.

━━ ━━ ━━

At the end of a footbridge in a marsh a few hundred metres from Nandikadal lagoon, a huge statue of a Sinhalese soldier rises,

Sri Lankan Army victory monument, Mullaitivu

a machine gun in one hand with a dove resting on it, the national flag in the other. Beneath his torso is an assembly of rocks engraved with battalion, division and squadron numbers of the units engaged in the genocidal final offensives through 2008-09. The army calls it "Victory Monument in Victorious Land". Concrete lions sit adjacent to the corners of its square base. "Sinhala" derives from the Sanskrit *Simha* ("lion"). In Buddhist mythology, the Sinhalese are lion people destined to rule the island. The symbolism is not lost in the former heartlands of Tiger rule.

Grotesque displays of military triumphalism are everywhere across the Vanni. LTTE cemeteries have been desecrated, destroyed, and former Tiger bases turned into museums of "terrorism". Dozens of garrisons and state security installations now litter Tamil Eelam. A large stone monument in front of one of the half dozen on the road from Jaffna to Mannar reads: "One nation One country". It is a command rather than a description. The military controls much of civilian and economic life here. It also exercises more insidious forms of control such as running pre-schools in the northern province. How must it be to look on as one's children and grandchildren are raised in the institutions of the oppressor nation. The Jaffna-based Adayaalam Centre for Policy Research and the Washington, DC-based People for Equality and Relief in Lanka estimate at least one soldier for every two civilians in Mullaitivu and note the "creation of economic dependency on the military; suppression of civic activism and destruction of community identity; and further marginalisation of women" across the Vanni.

This reality conflicts with official narratives from Colombo. In 2015, Rajapaksa was defeated by one-time ally Maithripala Sirisena in the presidential elections. Sirisena positioned himself as a reforming figure. His manifesto, *A compassionate Maithri governance – a stable country*, pledged to devolve executive presidential power to a new parliament and rewrite the constitution.

But, rejecting any international investigation into war crimes committed during the final stages of the war, Sirisena promised to protect Rajapaksa and army top brass. The promise of political change resulted in Tamils backing the challenger. The new president slightly eased the repression, which opened a limited political space for Tamil activists to re-group. But the occupation merely shifted gear.

The army's move into the civil economy, even if troop reductions eventually occur, is entrenching the Sinhalisation of Tamil Eelam, giving a pretext to reject Tamil claims for self-determination. The government's "facts on the ground" strategy is like the settler-colonialism of Israel in Palestine and Indonesia in West Papua. Capital from Colombo crowds out Tamil enterprises. Signs and street names are often in Sinhalese; thousands from the south have been brought into the Vanni and planted with state support on Tamil lands. This is the overarching goal of the chauvinists: to destroy the Tamil nation demographically and culturally.

"Today you are brought here and given a plot of land. You have been uprooted from your village. You are like a piece of driftwood in the ocean; but remember that one day the whole country will look up to you", Don Stephen Senanayake, the first prime minister of Ceylon, told Sinhala colonists in the southern Vanni in the 1950s. "The final battle for the Sinhala people will be fought [here]. You are men and women who will carry this island's destiny on your shoulders." More than thirty years later, Malinga Gunaratne, an architect of what he called a "pioneer army" that attempted mass migration of landless Sinhalese peasants to pierce the contiguity of Tamil Eelam, penned a bestselling work, *For a sovereign state*, now in its fifth edition.

"The cry for Eelam will cease only when the people of Sri Lanka belonging to all communities and races redistribute themselves in the northern and eastern parts of the country", he wrote. "The government today is labouring to settle two hundred thousand people

… What is required is a permanent solution. The permanent solution is to destroy the very foundation of the Eelam Raj … This could be done by taking out the eastern province, particularly Trincomalee, out of their map, and by strengthening the frontier Sinhala settlements … The strategy needs to be to spread population northwards from a well-established high population density centre."

Gunaratne painted a picture of a future state in which each lived alongside the other, regardless of ethnicity, language or religion. But not once did he acknowledge the oppression of Tamils. His multicultural narrative time and again was betrayed by the central thrust of the chauvinists' case. Mimicking the arguments of Zionists in Palestine, they portray the Sinhalese as chosen people treading water in a perilous Tamil sea that threatens to drown the island at any moment. Gunaratne was assisted by a charismatic monk – the "Dimbulagala priest" Matara Kithalagama Sri Seelalan-kara – who marched the peasants into their promised land. "He was playing on the emotions of the Sinhala people", Gunaratne wrote. "'One race, one religion, one people', seemed to be his battle cry … He had thrown in the correct ingredients of religion, adventure and patriotism to move the settlers."

In Jaffna, a doctor speaks at length about the demographic question. He says that the historic significance of the LTTE was not simply its achievements in advancing equality, but the defensive achievement of what he calls the "Tiger Wall". For nearly thirty years, the colonising invaders were held at bay by the guerrillas. The doctor, who was not a Tiger cadre, does not want to dwell, at least not today, on the army's 2009 genocidal offensive. The mass demographic engineering, a silent genocide, is, he says, the greatest crime. The military could never kill every individual in the north and the east – but the Tamil nation may be wiped out through peaceful means. Slow suffocation rather than imminent shelling is the risk now. In this, the human rights narratives of the NGOs and the UN, which focus only on the physical violence of the Sri Lankan state, are failing to acknowledge the insidious Sinhalisation project.

— — —

It's Maaveerar Naal (Heroes' Day) in Kilinochchi. The Tiger insignia is banned by the government, but hundreds of red and yellow flags flutter in defiance overhead and around the perimeter of a paddock on the town's western edge. This once was an LTTE burial ground. The remains of the bulldozed tombstones have been gathered into a small mountain of rock and cement, a monument to fallen Tiger soldiers. This is one of the most important events of the last seven years, possible only because the government recently lifted its ban on commemorations of this date.

Heroes' Day was first celebrated by the Tigers on 27 November 1989, the anniversary of the first LTTE combat death – lieutenant Shankar in 1982. The translator's absence makes it impossible to decipher the content of the speeches, which are solemn. Just after six o'clock, people light lanterns and candles. Proceedings end with the echo of a gong broadcast through loudspeakers. There are no chants; no raised fists – only remembrance and mourning. Photos of loved ones are displayed at the base of stakes in the ground surrounded by candles and garlands around which families congregate. Mothers sit quietly, or lie and weep, next to pictures of their sons. If there is political organising here, it is conducted in whispers.

The Tamils were pushed into a corner from which armed resistance seemed the only way out. They fought heroically but, in the end, the Tigers could not match the combined might of global imperialism. So what next for an oppressed people? The armed struggle has no future as a strategic approach: the weaponry and technology available to the state are too advanced for another national liberation war to be anything other than a suicide mission. The unavoidable fact is that Eelam Tamils have found themselves friendless. Successive Sri Lankan governments, the Buddhist clerical order, the left parties in the south, the parliamentary collaborators, the international "community" – all have proven to be enemies of emancipation. The crushing of the Tigers has set back the liberation struggle by at least a generation, maybe longer. Yet grassroots organising is increasing, with permanent protests not only for the disappeared, but for land rights at northern villages such as Keppapilavu and the small island of Iranaitivu. How these protests can be generalised and grow in the coming years is an open question – but only in collective struggle is there a future for the nation.

"At the moment, there is a big focus from the international community, primarily the Western states, on human rights and 'good governance'", a former Tiger cadre says. "These issues are being raised through the UN Human Rights Council. However, they are distracting from the key issues. Many Tamils have been putting false hope into these UN institu-

tions. The key issues need to be clearly focused on: the withdrawal of the Sri Lankan military, an end to the Sinhala-Buddhist colonisation schemes and a recognition of the right of Tamils as a national group and our right to self-determination in Tamil Eelam."

The one logical ally of the Tamils remains the impoverished Sinhalese workers and peasants in the south. Over the last sixty years, as Tamils struggled for recognition, these Sinhalese also suffered at the hands of the state and watched as their own leaders grew wealthy while the majority remained desperately poor. It remains the island's greatest political catastrophe that the once powerful Sinhalese left failed to stand with the Tamils and launch a united fight for the liberation of all exploited and oppressed people in Ceylon.

As dusk turns to night, a sacrificial flame radiates from a gold cauldron atop a wooden pylon near the monument of shattered tombstones. Past it file families and mourners, pausing to pay respects to their martyrs. Each

Recovered tombstone, Heroes' Day

takes a handful of flower petals to release and let float to the dirt. The flickering of the fire endures long after the procession has passed, and a question lingers as the hours go by: will this land once more burn with the fury of its youth, or will it rage only against the dying of the light?

1 The Permanent Peoples' Tribunal on Sri Lanka, held in 2013, concluded that genocide had been committed against the Eelam Tamils. Further, it ruled that the genocide is ongoing because of the continuing persecution in terms of arrests, torture, disappearances and land grabbing, and because more and more of the remaining cultural and geographic elements of Tamil Eelam are being replaced by Sinhala and Buddhist names and iconography.

2 Not his real name.

LIBERATION TIGERS AND TAMIL EELAM FREEDOM STRUGGLE

Political committee of the Liberation Tigers of Tamil Eelam, August 1983
Written by A.S. Balasingham
Statistics supplied by S. Subramanian

Note: this document has been slightly edited for clarity and to remove maps and statistical tables. Its inclusion is not an endorsement of the politics, strategy or tactics of the Liberation Tigers of Tamil Eelam. It is published for its historical value as one of the most comprehensive outlines of the thinking of a section of the Tiger leadership in the early phase of its war of national liberation.

INTRODUCTION

National Liberation struggles are being fought on several fronts of the world today. Oppressed peoples and nations are waging a determined struggle against imperialism, against neo-colonialism, against Zionism, against racism and many other forms of oppression. Each of these revolutionary struggles has its own historical specificity, its own concrete conjunctural situations, which determine the strategy and tactics of each of these liberation struggles. Within the specificity and particularity of these struggles lies the universal historical principle of the socialist revolutionary doctrine – that it is the oppressed masses who are the potential revolutionary force, the historical force, and that it is the oppressed who create history and change the world.

Within the context of this historical law of social development and transformation, the Marxist-Leninist theoretical and political framework recognises that the national liberation struggle of any oppressed nation is progressive in essence and has revolutionary potential if it is articulated in the sphere of democratic struggle and proletarian revolution. The right of nations to self-determination, in Lenin's formulation, is a realistic, revolutionary theory which upholds the universal socialist principle of the fundamental right of a nation to secede and form a state of its own, a principle aimed to protect a small nation from the oppression generated from the national chauvinism of a big nation, a principle designed to preserve a nation's cultural and ethnic identity, a principle, if adhered to truly and fairly, that can create the necessary conditions for proletarian internationalism.

The Tamil national question in Sri Lanka is being fought on the basis of that nation's right to self-determination. For the last thirty-five years the nation of Tamil Eelam has been subjected to severe oppression. It took the form of a violent oppression perpetrated against a small nation by the national chauvinism of a big nation, the Sinhala nation, the ruling elites of which pursued a disastrous policy aimed at destroying the ethnic identity of the Tamil speaking people and threatened their very survival. For nearly a quarter of a century Tamil parliamentary political parties launched non-violent campaigns of satyagraha seeking the restoration of basic human rights. Yet the civilized political demands of the Tamils were met with a savage form of military repression, the promises given to them never fulfilled, and the agreements and pacts became dead letters. The national friction between the two nations finally emerged as a major contradiction leading to the demand for secession by the oppressed.

To the world community, the Sri Lankan ruling class portrays the country as a tranquil island, cherishing the Buddhist ideals of peace and Dharma and adhering to a harmless political doctrine of non-alignment. Paradoxically, behind this political facade lies the factual reality, the reality of national oppression, of the blatant violation of basic human rights, of racial crimes, of police and military violence, of attempted genocide. Masterminding the worst form of capitalist exploitative machinery under the slogans of democracy and socialism, the Sinhala ruling class since independence had always reinforced their political power with an abominable ideology of national chauvinism and religious fanaticism. By utilising such ideological apparatus and by actually practising a calculated policy of genocidal oppression, the ruling bourgeoisie has been able to maintain its domination over the proletariat of the oppressor nation and prevented the class unity between the Sinhalese and Tamils. Yet on the other hand, Sinhala chauvinism and its violent manifestations have helped the polarisation of the heterogeneous masses of the oppressed Tamil nation, with different class elements and castes, towards a determined revolutionary struggle for political independence.

The struggle for national freedom having failed in its democratic popular agitations, having exhausted its power to mobilise the masses for peaceful campaigns, gave rise to the emergence of an armed resistance movement in Tamil Eelam in the early seventies. Armed resistance as a mode of popular struggle arose when our people were presented with no alternative other than to resort to revolutionary resistance to defend themselves against a savage form of state terrorism. The armed struggle, therefore, is the historical product of intolerable national oppression; it is an extension, continuation and advancement of the political struggle of our oppressed people. Our liberation movement, which spearheads the revolutionary armed struggle in Tamil Eelam, is the vanguard of the national struggle. The armed struggle of our liberation movement is sustained and supported by wider sections of the Tamil masses, since our revolutionary political project expresses the profound aspirations of our people to gain political independence from the autocratic domination and repression of the Sri Lankan state. To achieve the revolutionary tasks of national emancipation and socialist revolution, our project aims at the extension and transformation of our protracted guerrilla warfare into a people's war of national liberation.

This political document attempts to introduce the national liberation struggle of the people of Tamil Eelam to the progressive world. It also documents the historical genesis of our revolutionary liberation organisation; it briefly specifies our theoretical perspective, political programme of action and military strategies. The first part of this work sketches a brief history of our nation and outlines the multiple dimensions of the racist oppression aimed at the structural destruction of our national foundations. The second part of the document details the non-violent political struggles of the Tamil bourgeois parliamentary party and the emergence of revolutionary armed resistance. The final part discusses the question of self-determination and the polit-ico-military objectives of our movement. By providing the historical background and analysing the concrete conditions of our unique situation, we argue that our armed revolutionary struggle for national independence is progressive, revolutionary and solidly based on the revolutionary political praxis of Marxism and Leninism.

PART ONE: MULTIPLE OPPRESSIONS WITH GENOCIDAL INTENT

Historical background: two nations on one island

The island formerly called Ceylon is the traditional homeland of two nations – Tamil Eelam and Sri Lanka, two distinct social formations with distinct cultures and languages having their own unique historical past. The history of the Tamils on the island dates back to pre-historic times. When the ancestors of the Sinhala people arrived in the Island with their legendary Prince Vijaya from northern India in the 6th century BC, Dravidians (Tamils) were living on the island. Though the question of original settlement is obscured by legends and mythologies, modern scholars hold that Tamils were indisputably the earliest settlers. The Sinhalese historical chronicles, "Mahawamsa" and "Culawamsa", record the turbulent historical past of the island from the 6th century BC, the history of great wars between Tamil and Sinhalese kings, of invasions from South Indian Tamil empires, of struggles for supremacy between Tamil and Sinhalese kingdoms. The island was ruled by the Tamil kings at times and then by the Sinhalese kings, and the intermittent wars forced the Sinhalese kings to move their capital southwards. From the 13th century onwards until the advent of foreign colonialism, the Tamils lived as a stable national entity in their own kingdom ruled by their own kings, within a specified territory of their traditional homelands embracing the northern and eastern provinces.

Marco Polo once described Sri Lanka as the island paradise of the earth. The British used to call it the "pearl of the Indian Ocean". Separated from the southern coast of India only by a twenty-two mile stretch of water, the island has an area of 25,332 square miles. For centuries before the colonial penetration, the island had a traditional self-sustaining economy with a reputation of being the granary of the east. The mode of production in the pre-colonial epoch is feudal in character with dying elements of the Asiatic mode. Structured within the feudal mode, the economic organisation of the Tamil nation had a unique set of relations of production characterised by caste stratification with its hierarchy of functions. The extensive hydraulic system, with its network of tanks and canals for which the mediaeval Ceylon was famous, had fallen out of use and was decaying and disappearing under the thick jungles in the north as well as in the north-central provinces. The Sinhalese feudal aristocracy, by this time, had moved to the central highlands and established Kandy as the capital.

When the Portuguese first landed on the island in the beginning of the 16th century, they found two ancient kingdoms, Tamils in the north and eastern provinces and the Sinhalese in the south, two distinct social systems with different cultures, constituting themselves as separate nations of people ruled by their own kings with independent state structures. The Portuguese entered into treaties, and then fought battles, and finally, in the battle of 1619, they conquered the Tamil kingdom and hanged the Tamil king Sankili Kumaran. Yet the Portuguese, and the Dutch who came after them, governed the Tamil nation as a separate kingdom without violating the territorial integrity until the British, in 1833, brought a unified state structure amalgamating the two nations irrespective of ethnic differences, laying the foundation for the present national conflict.

Plantation economy and the Tamil workers

The effects of Portuguese and Dutch colonial rule on the island's pre-capitalist economic formation is minimal when compared to the profound effects of British imperialist domination. The most significant historical event of the British imperial rule was the imposition of an exploitative plantation economy.

It was in 1815, with the conquest of the Kandyan kingdom by the British, that the painful history of the Tamil plantation worker begins. It is during this time that British imperialism decided to introduce the colonial plantation economy in the island. Coffee plantations were set up in the early 1820s, a crop which flourished in high altitudes. Speculators and entrepreneurs from England rushed to the newly conquered mountain areas and expropriated vast tracts of land, by deceit, from the Kandyan peasantry. The Kandyan peasants refused to abandon their traditional subsistent holdings to become wage-earners on these new capitalist estates. The pressure exerted by the colonial state to draw the labour power from the indigenous Sinhalese peasantry did not work. The British imperialist masters were thus compelled to draw on its limitless reserve army of labour from India. A massive army of cheap labourers were conscripted from southern India, who, partly by their own poverty and partly by coercion, moved into this promised land to be condemned to an appalling form of slave labour. A notorious system of labour contract was established which allowed hundreds of thousands of Tamil labourers to migrate to the plantation estates. In the 1840s and 1850s, a million people were imported. The original workers were recruited from Tamil Nadu districts of Tinnevely, Madurai and Tanjore and were from the poor, oppressed castes. This army of recruited workers were forced to walk hundreds of miles from their villages to Rameswaram and again from Mannar to the central highlands of Ceylon through impenetrable jungles. Thousands of these immiserated masses perished on their long, hazardous journey, a journey chartered with disease, death and despair. Those who survived the journey were weak and exhausted, and thousands of them died in the nightmarish unhealthy conditions of the early plantations.

The coffee plantation economy collapsed in the 1870s when a leaf disease ravaged the plantations. But the economic system survived

intact by the introduction of a successor crop – tea. Tea was introduced in the 1880s on a wider scale. The tea plantation economy
expanded with British entrepreneurial investments, export markets
and consolidated companies transforming the structure of production
and effectively changing the economic foundation of the old feudal
mode, creating the basis for the development of the capitalist mode
of production. Though the plantation economy effectively changed
the process of production, the Tamil labourers – men, women and
children – were permanently condemned to slave under the white
masters and the indigenous capitalists. The British planters who
brought the Indian Tamil labourers into Sri Lanka deliberately seg-
regated them inside the plantations in what are known as the "line
rooms". Such a notorious policy of segregation condemned the Tamils
permanently into these miserable ghettos, isolated them from the rest
of the population and prevented them from buying their own lands,
building their own houses and leading a free social existence. Thus,
British imperialism built up the Tamil plantation proletariat within
the heartland of the Kandyan Sinhalese and manipulated the Tamil/
Sinhala antagonism to divide and rule and to defeat the class struggle.
Reduced to a condition of slavery by colonialism, the Tamil plantation
workers toiled in utter misery; their sweat and blood sustained the
worst form of exploitative economy that fed the imperialist vampires
with the surplus value and enriched the Sinhalese landowning classes.

British colonialism and the indigenous Tamils

The impact of the British imperial domination on the indigenous
Tamil speaking people of the northern and eastern provinces had far
reaching effects. On the political level, British imperialism imposed
a unified administration with centralised institutions, establishing a
singular state structure which ended the separate existence of the Tamil
statehood. This forceful annexation and amalgamation of two separate

kingdoms, of two nations of people, disregarding their past historical existence, their socio-cultural distinctions, and their ethnic differences was the root cause of the present Tamil-Sinhala antagonism.

The Tamil social formation was constituted by a unique socio-economic organisation, in which feudal elements and caste system were tightly interwoven to form the foundation of this complex society. The notorious system of caste stratification bestows, by right of birth, power, privilege and status to the high caste Tamils, the minority of whom (landowners and business elites) owned the means of production and exploited the rest. The most exploited and oppressed sections are the so-called depressed castes who eke out a banal existence under this system of slavery. Privileged by caste and provided with better educational facilities created by foreign missionaries, a section of the high caste Tamils adopted the English educational system. A new class of English-educated professionals and white collar workers emerged and became a part of the bureaucratic structure of the civil service. The English imperialist masters encouraged the Tamils and provided them with an adequate share in the state administration under a notorious strategy of balance of power, of divide and rule, that later sparked the fires of Sinhala national chauvinism.

Tamil dominance in the state administrative structure and in the plantation economic sector, the privileges enjoyed by the English-educated elites and the spread of Christianity are factors that propelled the emergence of Sinhala nationalism. In the early stages, nationalist tendencies took the form of Buddhist revival, which gradually assumed a powerful political dominance. Under the slogan of Buddhist religious renaissance, a national chauvinistic ideology emerged with strong sediments of Tamil antagonism. The religious leadership attacked both the Tamils and European colonialists and spoke of the greatness of the Sinhalese Aryan race. To quote a typical example:

"Ethnologically, the Sinhalese are a unique race, inasmuch as they can boast that they have no slave blood in them, and were never conquered by either the pagan Tamils or European vandals who for three centuries devastated the land, destroyed ancient temples … and nearly annihilated the historic race. This bright, beautiful island was made into a paradise by the Aryan Sinhalese before its destruction was brought about by the barbaric vandals." (Anagarika Dharmapala, *History of an ancient civilization*)

The Sinhala national chauvinism that emerged from the Buddhist religious resurgence viewed the Tamil dominance in the state apparatus and in the plantation economy as a threat to "national development". Such national antagonism articulated on the ideological level began to take concrete forms of social, political and economic oppression soon after national independence in 1948, when state power was transferred to the Sinhala national bourgeoisie.

Multi-dimensional oppression

Having firmly entrenched the national bourgeoisie in a global neo-colonial structure, the British granted "independence" to the people of Sri Lanka and Tamil Eelam with the British queen as their sovereign head. Motivated by their class interests, the national bourgeoisie collaborated with the British, accepted their constitution and assumed power. Soon after the so-called national independence, the national bourgeoisie began to show its reactionary character. Conflicts arose between the Tamil and Sinhala bourgeoisie over the share of political power. The Sinhala nationalists dominated the scene and gained control over the state machinery.

Soon after the transfer of political power, Sinhala national chauvinism reigned supreme and unleashed a vicious and violent form of oppression against the Tamils. This oppression has a continuous history of thirty-five years since "independence" and has been practised by successive Sri Lankan governments. The oppression has a genocidal intent involving a calculated plan aiming at the gradual and systematic destruction of the essential foundations of the Tamil national community. This oppression therefore assumed a multi-dimensional thrust, attacking simultaneously on different levels the conditions of existence of the Tamil speaking nation; on language, on education, on culture, on religious and political institutions, on traditional lands and on the economy that jeopardised the very existence of the Tamils and made unitary life intolerable and impossible. As a part of this genocidal programme formed the state-organised racial holocausts, which constantly plague the island, resulting in mass extermination of Tamils and massive destruction of Tamil property.

A million Tamil workers disenfranchised

Soon after the transfer of political power, Sinhala national chauvinism reigned supreme, and the first cruel victims of the Sinhala racist onslaught were the Tamil plantation workers. A million of this working mass who toiled for the prosperity of the island for more than a century were disenfranchised by the most infamous citizenship legislations in Sri Lankan political history, which robbed these people of their basic human rights and reduced them to an appalling condition of statelessness. Having been deprived of the right of political participation, the state parliament was closed for this huge mass of working people. Before the introduction of these laws, the plantation Tamils were represented by seven members of parliament. In the general elections of 1952, a direct consequence of these citizenship laws, not a single representative could be returned.

The Citizenship Act of 1948 and the Indian Pakistani Citizenship Act of 1949 laid down stringent conditions for the acquisition of citizenship by descent as well as by virtue of residence for a stipulated period. These Acts were implemented in such a manner that only about 130,000 out of more than a million people were able to acquire citizenship. The cumulative effects of these notorious legislations were so disastrous that they made the conditions of life of these working people miserable and tragic. Having been reduced to a condition of statelessness, nearly a million Tamils were denied the right to participate in local and national elections; were denied employment opportunities in the public and private sectors; were denied the right to purchase lands; were denied the right to enter business of any sort. Such a condition of statelessness condemned this entire mass of workers, the classical proletariat of the island, into a dehumanised class devoid of any rights and dumped them perpetually in their plantation ghettos to suffer degradation and despair.

Aggressive annexation and colonisation of traditional lands

The most vicious form of oppression calculated to destroy the national identity of the Tamils was the state-aided aggressive colonisation which began soon after the "independence" and has now swallowed nearly three thousand square miles of Tamil Eelam. This planned occupation of Tamil lands by hundreds of thousands of Sinhala people, aided and abetted by the Sinhala colonial regime in the areas where a huge mass of landless Tamil peasantry is striving for a tiny plot to toil, was aimed to annihilate the geographical entity of the Tamil nation and to reduce the Tamils to a minority in their own historical lands. The worst affected areas are in the eastern province. The gigantic Gal Oya and Madura Oya development schemes have robbed huge bulks of land from the Tamil speaking people of Islamic faith of Batticaloa district. The colonisation scheme in Allai and Kantalai and the Yan Oya project have engulfed the Trincomalee area, which threatens to be swallowed by Sinhala colonisation. The Mahaveli development scheme is planned to penetrate the north with massive Sinhala colonisation. This consistent policy of forceful annexation of Tamil traditional lands exposes the vicious nature of the racist policies of the Sinhala ruling classes.

The state-aided colonisation has not only created two new Sinhala electorates (Amparai and Seruwilla), but also threatens to cut off geographically the eastern province from the north. In addition to this, the constant racial violence that erupts in some sensitive colonised areas has resulted in heavy loss of Tamil life and property. In the June-July (1983) racial holocaust, the Sinhalese colonists, with the aid of the armed forces, launched calculated attacks on the Tamil people of Trincomalee to confiscate their property and to drive them away from their traditional homelands. In 1948, there were only ten thousand Sinhalese in the eastern province, which has swelled by 1977 to over one hundred thousand people. In Amparai district, the percentage of the Sinhalese population was 4.5 percent in 1946, but increased to 37.7 percent recently.

The assault on language and the axe on employment

The national oppression of the Sinhala racist regimes soon penetrated into the sphere of language, education and employment. The chauvinist "Sinhala Only" movement spearheaded by Mr S.W.R.D. Bandaranayake [founder of the nationalist Sri Lanka Freedom Party and fourth prime minister of Ceylon] brought him to political power in 1956. His first Act in parliament put an end to the official equal status enjoyed by the Tamil language and made Sinhala as the only official language of the country. The "Sinhala Only Act" demanded proficiency in Sinhala in the civil service. The Tamil public servants, deprived of the rights of increments and promotions, were forced to learn the language or leave employment. Employment opportunities in the public service were practically closed to Tamils. Racial discrimination against the Tamils in employment soon extended to other services and sectors.

The arrest on education

Education was the sphere that Sinhala chauvinism struck deeply to deprive a vast population of Tamil youth access to higher education and employment. A notorious discriminatory selective device called "standardisation" was introduced in 1970, which demanded higher merits of marks from the Tamil students for university admissions whereas the Sinhalese students were admitted with lower grades. This discriminatory device dramatically reduced the number of admissions of Tamil students and seriously undermined their prospects of higher studies.

The present regime withdrew the scheme of standardisation temporarily in 1978 but has reintroduced a new discriminatory formula (admitting 30 percent on merit, 55 percent on district basis and 15 percent from backward areas). This new scheme turns out to be far more discriminatory than the earlier one, denying thousands of deserving Tamil students the right of higher education. Angered by the imposition of an alien language, frustrated without the possibility of higher education, plunged into the despair of unemployed existence, the Tamil youth grew militant with an iron determination to fight back the national oppression.

Economic strangulation of the Tamil nation

National oppression showed its intensity in the economic strangulation of the Tamil Eelam nation. Apart from a few state-owned factories built soon after "independence", Tamil areas were totally isolated from all the national development projects for nearly thirty-five years. While the Sinhala nation flourished with massive development projects, the Tamil nation was alienated as an unwanted colony, isolated into the wilderness of economic deprivation. The most tragic fact is that while the Tamil nation gradually deteriorated into economic backwardness, wasting its potential productive labour, the Tamil capitalists, encouraged and aided by the Sinhala ruling class, invested in the south; a brutal fact that illustrates the class collaboration and class interests of the Tamil bourgeoisie.

Racial riots and mass killings of Tamils

The racial riots that constantly plague the island should not be viewed as spontaneous outbursts of inter-communal hatred between the two communities. All major conflagrations that erupted violently against the Tamil people were inspired and masterminded by the Sinhala ruling regimes as a part of a genocidal programme. Violent anti-Tamil racial riots exploded in 1956, 1958, 1961, 1974, 1977, 1979, 1981 and most recently in July this year. In these racial holocausts, thousands of Tamils, including women and children, were mercilessly massacred in the most gruesome manner, millions worth of Tamil property was destroyed and hundreds of thousands made refugees. The state and the armed forces colluded with hooligans and vandals in their sadistic orgy of arson, rape and mass murders.

The cumulative effect of this multi-dimensional oppression threatened the very survival of the Tamils. It aggravated the national conflict and made co-existence between the two nations intolerable. It has shattered all hopes of a peaceful negotiated resolution of the Tamil national question. It has stiffened the Tamil militancy in their demand for secession.

PART TWO: TAMIL NATIONAL FREEDOM STRUGGLE

The emergence of Tamil nationalism and the Federal Party

Tamil nationalism arose as a historical consequence of Sinhala chauvinistic oppression. As the collective sentiment of the oppressed people, Tamil nationalism constituted progressive and revolutionary elements. It is progressive since it expressed the profound aspirations of the oppressed masses for freedom, dignity and justice. It has a revolutionary character since it was able to mobilise all sections of the popular masses and poised them for a political battle for national freedom. Tamil national sentiments found organisational expression in the Federal Party, which emerged as a powerful political force in 1956 to spearhead the Tamil national movement. Structurally, it was a nationalist party founded on a conservative ideology, with bourgeois and petty bourgeois class elements and interests dominating the leadership. As a national movement championing the cause of the Tamil nation, the party did contain progressive and democratic contents and was able to organise and mobilise various strata of classes and castes into a huge mass movement.

The failure of the left movement to establish a strong political base among the working masses of the Tamil nation was due to their lack of political vision in comprehending and situating the concrete conditions of national oppression. Positing the class struggle over and against the national struggle of an oppressed nation, they conceived the national patriotic upsurge of the Tamil masses as the manifestation of reactionary bourgeois nationalism, ignoring the progressive and revolutionary potential of the struggle. Their lack of theoretical perspective in this crucial domain allowed them to speak of proletarian internationalism without realising the political reality that national oppression is the enemy of the class struggle and that proletarian solidarity is practically unattainable when national oppression presents itself as the major contradiction between the two nations. The success of the Federal Party in securing popular mass support lies in the fact that they apprehended the onslaught of Sinhala national chauvinism against the Tamil nation. The thrust of the multi-dimensional oppression, the leadership perceived, would jeopardise the identity and cohesiveness of the Tamil national totality. Warning of this impending danger, they campaigned and organised all sections of the Tamil masses, invoking the spirit of nationalism. The party thus emerged as a powerful national movement polarising the formless conglomeration of classes and castes into a huge mass movement poised for massive democratic struggles.

A broken pact

The adamant determination of the chauvinistic bourgeois government of Mr Bandaranayake to implement the racist Sinhala Only Act became a crucial political challenge to the Federal Party, which decided to launch a satyagraha campaign (passive, peaceful, sit-in protest of Gandhian non-violent method) as a form of popular resistance. It was on the morning of 5 June 1956 when parliament assembled to debate the Sinhala Only Act. The Federal Party parliamentarians, party members and sympathisers in hundreds performed satyagraha on the Galle Face Green, just opposite the parliament building. Within hours, the satyagrahis were mobbed by thousands of hooligans and vandals who stoned, assaulted the peaceful pickets. When the situation became uncontrollable and dangerous, the Federal Party leaders called off the protest. The rioters, who harassed the satyagrahis, went on a bloodthirsty rampage in the city, assaulting Tamils and looting Tamil property. The riot soon spread to several parts of the island, with violent incidents of murder, looting, arson and rape. At Amparai, more than a hundred

Tamils were massacred. Irrespective of the spreading communal violence and the Tamil protest campaign, the Sinhala Only Bill was passed and the Tamil language lost its official status.

Following the implementation of the Sinhala Only Act, the Federal Party organised mass agitational campaigns demanding a federal form of autonomy for the Tamil nation. In the elections of 1956, the party won an overwhelming victory, obtaining a clear mandate from the Tamil people for a federal form of self-government. The party also made a decision to intensify the satyagraha campaign to achieve its demands. The demand for political autonomy for the Tamil nation, along with the rising wave of Tamil nationalism, alarmed the Sinhala ruling elite. Mr Bandaranayake, in a desperate attempt to arrest the growing conflict, agreed to give concessions to the Tamils. A pact was signed between him and the Federal Party leader Mr S.J.V. Chelvanayagam, which provided some elements of political autonomy under regional councils, with a promise to stop Sinhala colonisation of Tamil areas. The pact sparked off suspicion and resentment among the Sinhalese racialist elements, and the man who exploited this situation at that time was none other than the present fascist dictator, J.R. Jayawardene [United National Party leader and first executive president under the 1978 constitution], who, with the support of the Buddhist monks, organised a massive protest march to Kandy demanding the abrogation of the pact. This Sinhala chauvinistic upsurge inspired some ministers of Mr Bandaranayake's cabinet to organise a protest of their own against the pact. Led by these ministers, a long procession of Bhikkus and their racist sympathisers marched to the prime minister's residence carrying a copy of the pact in a coffin. The communal drama finally ended with the ceremonial burning of the coffin in front of Rosemead Place, where Mr Bandaranayake made a solemn pledge to abrogate the pact.

The racist horror of 1958

This great betrayal by the Sinhala national bourgeoise blew up all hopes of a national harmony, and the relations between the two nations became hostile. The national friction gradually became intense and exploded into violent racial riots in 1958. This communal fury that ravaged throughout the island stained the pages of Ceylon's history with blood. The horror and savagery perpetrated against the innocent Tamils are indescribable. Several hundreds were butchered to death, hundreds of thousands lost their homes, and several millions worth of Tamil property were either looted or burnt to ashes; Tamil children were hacked to death, pregnant women were raped and slaughtered; a Hindu priest was burnt alive.

Several mutilated bodies were found in a well at Maha Oya. At Kalutara, a Tamil family while attempting to hide in a well had petrol poured on them and, when they begged for mercy, they were set on fire. As the cries of agony arose when they were roasted alive in a huge ball of fire, the racist spectators were enthralled by sadistic ecstasy. While the whole island was being consumed by the flames of racial horror, Mr Bandaranayake watched this tragic holocaust with amusement and refused to declare a state of emergency until the Tamils, as he was reported to have said, "get a taste of it". After twenty-four hours of calculated delay, a state of emergency was declared. When the situation was brought under control, there were ten thousand Tamil refugees, most of them civil servants, professionals and businessmen, who had to be shipped to the northern and eastern provinces, the historical motherland of the Tamils.

The satyagraha campaign

The 1958 racial holocaust cut a deep wedge in the relations between the Tamil and Sinhala nations. Tamil national sentiments ran high and erupted into massive agitational campaigns in the Tamil political arena. It was in the early part of 1961 that the Federal Party decided to launch direct action in the form of satyagraha in front of government offices in the northern and eastern provinces. The objective was to disrupt and disorganise the government's administrative structure in Tamil Eelam, thereby exerting pressure on the government to accept the Tamil demand for federal autonomy.

The satyagraha campaign of 1961 was a monumental event in the history of the Tamil national struggle. The campaign unfolded into a huge upsurge of the popular Tamil masses to register a national protest against the oppressive policies of the Sinhala ruling elites. This civil disobedience campaign, which was inaugurated on 20 February 1961 and lasted nearly three months, brought hundreds of thousands of Tamil speaking masses into the streets to express their defiance and dissent to the oppressive state apparatus. Within a couple of weeks, the whole government administrative machinery was paralysed and the Tamil nation was practically cut off from any authority of the central government. This unprecedented historical event symbolised national solidarity; it symbolised the collective will and determination of the whole nation to assert its national identity and independence.

The campaign started as a massive picketing in front of the government's main administrative office, Kachcheri, in Jaffna, the northern capital, and soon spread to Vavuniya, Mullaitivu, Mannar, Trincomalee and Batticaloa and other towns. All sections of the Tamil speaking people, irrespective of religion and caste, enthusiastically participated in this peaceful popular protest. Thousands of Tamil plantation workers from the south converged into the north and east to express their militant solidarity. This massive national uprising encouraged the Federal Party leadership to open a postal service on 14 April 1961, and Tamil national stamps were issued in thousands as an act of defiance against the state authority.

Alarmed by the rising tide of Tamil nationalism and the extraordinary success of the civil disobedience campaign, the state oppressive machinery reacted swiftly, mobilising the military into action. Large contingents of armed forces were dispatched to Tamil areas with "special instructions" under emergency powers. In the early hours of

18 April 1961, troops suddenly swooped on the satyagrahis in Jaffna and brutally attacked them with rifle butts and batons, fracturing their skulls and limbs. This barbarous military violence unleashed against the non-violent agitators resulted in hundreds of them sustaining serious injuries. Under the guise of emergency and curfew, military terrorism was let loose all over Tamil Eelam, supressing the agitation with brutal violence. The nationalist leaders were arrested, the party offices ransacked and the situation, in the government's view, "was brought under control". Thus, the violence of the oppressor silenced the non-violence of the oppressed; the armed might of Sinhala chauvinism crushed the "ahimsa" [non-violence] of Tamils. This historical event marked the beginning of a political experience that was crucial to the Tamil national struggle, an experience that taught the Tamils that the moral power of non-violence could not consume the military power of a violent oppressor whose racial hatred transcends all ethical norms of humanness and civilised behaviour. To the oppressor, this event encouraged the view that military terrorism is the only answer to the Tamil demand and that the non-violent foundation of the Tamil political agitation is a weak and impotent structure against the barrel of the gun.

Another broken pact

In 1965, the Sinhala national bourgeois party, the United National Party (UNP), assumed political power. The Federal Party decided to collaborate with this so-called national government with the expectation of wrenching some concessions for the Tamils. This collaborationist strategy, the Tamil leadership vainly hoped, would bring a negotiated settlement to the Tamil question. The UNP government, in a treacherous move to placate the Tamil nationalists, appointed a senior Federal Party member to its cabinet and in the following year promulgated regulations defining certain uses of the Tamil language in the transaction of government business. A secret pact was also made between Mr Chelvanayagam, the Federal Party leader, and the late [UNP leader] Mr Dudley Senanayake making provision for the establishment of district councils.

Neither the regulations for the use of Tamil language nor the promise of decentralisation of political power to regional bodies were implemented. The communal politics of the Sinhala bourgeoisie never allowed for a mechanism of negotiated settlement. It is an established historical pattern that when one party in power attempts a negotiated settlement to the Tamil question, the party in opposition invokes anti-Tamil sentiments to undermine the move, thereby scoring a political victory over the opponent as the heroes and guardians of Sinhala "patriotism". Caught up in this invariable political practice, the UNP government abrogated the pact when confronted with the pressure of Sinhala opposition. Thus, the collaborationist strategy of the Federal Party suffered the inevitable fate of betrayal and, in humiliation, the party withdrew its support for the government in 1968.

The Tamil political history from 1970 to 1977 contains the most outstanding events and unprecedented shifts. This historical epoch was characterised by heightened national oppression and increased youth rebellion against state domination, a conflict that intensified national contradiction, leading to the crystallisation of secessionist tendencies. Insofar as the Sinhala nation was concerned, this period consisted of events of great political betrayals and class collaborations, events of violent revolts and brutal reprisals. For both the oppressed Tamil nation and the suppressed Sinhala masses, this historical epoch, marked by the reign of an infamous regime, taught the most painful lessons of political oppression. The Tamil nation faced institutionalised oppression, and the decades of failures, frustration and exhaustion of struggles for regional autonomy led the nationalist leadership to move rapidly towards the inevitable choice of political independence. The working class movement as a whole suffered a tragic setback by the chauvinism of the ruling bourgeoisie and by the betrayal of the left leadership.

An alliance between the national bourgeois party, Mrs Sirima Bandaranayake's Sri Lanka Freedom Party (SLFP), and the traditional old left – the Trotskyite Lanka Sama Samaja Party (LSSP) and the Communist Party – brought to political power in 1970 what is mistakenly called the "Popular Front" government. As soon as the new government assumed power, it was confronted with a Sinhala youth insurrection. In an absurd and adventurous attempt to wrench power from the state, the newly formed Marxist militant organisation, the Janatha Vimukthi Peramuna (People's Liberation Front), rose in rebellion in the south. Thoroughly disorganised in the structure of its leadership and in the rank and file, ignoring the objective and subjective conditions of a revolutionary situation, the movement mobilised unemployed militant youth and sections of landless peasantry for a popular rebellion. Having established no political bases within the urban proletariat nor within the Tamil plantation proletariat, the real vanguard of a socialist revolution, having antagonised the Tamil nation as a whole by malicious communal propaganda, the movement in its infantile disorder embarked on a politico-military adventure the cost of which in human life was colossal.

This sudden uprising, which took the form of widespread armed rebellion, was met with the most barbaric military suppression in Sri Lankan history. To bring the situation under control, more than ten thousand Sinhalese youths were mercilessly slaughtered and another fifteen thousand imprisoned. This violent catastrophe wiped out a whole generation of radical Sinhala youth who sincerely believed that a revolutionary insurrection would redeem them from the misery and despair of unemployed existence. The rivers of blood that ran from these butchered innocents stained every inch of the Sinhala nation, the acclaimed holy land of compassionate Buddhism. The shame of history befell on those who masterminded this mass murder, on those ruling bourgeois who plotted to wipe out thousands of their own children to stabilise their political power and glory. Thus, this huge bloodbath was the major offer of "socialist humanism" pledged by the New "Left" Front. In its Hitlerian determination to wipe out by brutal force any further revolutionary upsurge emanating from the oppressed sections, the ruling elite enacted emergency laws and other repressive legislations and strengthened its grip on the state apparatus.

The Republican Constitution

Having suppressed the militant Sinhala youth, the new regime turned its oppressive apparatus towards the Tamils in an attempt to legalise and institutionalise national oppression. The most important measure in this respect was the adoption of a new Republican Constitution which reaffirmed the position that Sinhala was the sole official language and conferred a special status on Buddhism. The new constitution not only removed the fundamental rights, privileges and safeguards accorded to "national minorities" in the previous constitution, but also made S.W.R.D. Bandaranayake's racist pieces of legislation on language and religion as the supreme laws of the land.

Chapter three, Article seven, of the new constitution stated: "The official language of Sri Lanka shall be Sinhala as provided by the Official Language Act, No. 33 of 1956". The primacy of Buddhism was accorded in the following words: "The Republic of Sri Lanka shall give to Buddhism the foremost place and accordingly it shall be the duty of the state to protect and foster Buddhism while assuring to all religions the rights granted by Section 18(1)(d)".

The Constituent Assembly categorically rejected all amendments and resolutions proposed on behalf of the Tamil speaking people. A comprehensive federal scheme proposed by the Federal Party was turned down even without discussion. All efforts to secure a place in the new constitution for the use of Tamil language ended in fiasco. Sinhala national chauvinism reigned supreme in the deliberations of the assembly, which resulted in most of the Tamil members of parliament walking

116

out in utter frustration and haplessness. This infamous constitution, which was passed on 22 May 1972, brought an end to Tamil participation in the sharing of state power and created a condition of political alienation of a nation of people. Thus, the chauvinism of the Sinhala national bourgeoisie triggered off the causal mechanism precipitating the dynamics of a revolutionary rupture between two nations.

On the path to secession

The principal determinant factor that propelled the dynamics of national friction leading to the inevitable choice of political independence was none other than national oppression. The new constitution that alienated and expelled the Tamil nation from the structure of a unitary state climaxed this national contradiction.

It must be noted that for a period of nearly three decades, all bourgeois governments which represented the Sinhala nation – the UNP, the SLFP, the United Front of the SLFP, LSSP and CP – have consistently and deliberately denied the very basic human rights of the Tamil speaking people. Practically, almost all Sinhala political movements, including the Marxist parties, turned a deaf ear to the Tamil question. (For years, the Trotskyite LSSP and the Communist Party championed the rights of Tamils and maintained a commitment to parity of status for the Tamil language, but succumbed to political opportunism in the early '60s and shifted their position by supporting Sinhala Only/Buddhism Only chauvinism.) This unholy alliance of all major Sinhala political parties and their arrogant determination to stifle the most crucial and urgent issues facing the Tamil nation made the Tamils realise the utter futility of pursuing any form of rational political dialogue with Sinhala leaders. The consolidation of political forces of the Sinhala nation for a confrontation rather than coexistence with the Tamil nation forced the Tamil speaking masses to the inevitable position of deciding their own political destiny. These objective factors led to the polarisation and consolidation of Tamil political forces into a united national movement to struggle for a common cause – the independence of the Tamil nation. The major event in this direction took place at an all-party conference held at Trincomalee on 14 May 1972 in which the Federal Party, the Tamil Congress and the Ceylon Workers Congress of Mr Thondaman converged to form the Tamil United Front. This unprecedented move demonstrated the unity, cohesion and determination of the Tamil speaking people to fight to preserve their national identity and political liberty.

The militancy of the revolutionary youth

The most crucial factor that propelled the Tamil United Front to move rapidly towards the secessionist path was the increasing impatience, militancy and rebelliousness of the revolutionary Tamil youth. Disillusioned with the political strategy of non-violence, which the bourgeois nationalist readership advocated for the last thirty years and produced no political fruits, the Tamil youth demanded drastic and radical action for a swift resolution to the Tamil national question. Caught up in a revolutionary situation generated by the contradiction of national oppression, and constantly victimised by police brutality, the youth were forced to abandon the Gandhian doctrine of "ahimsa", which they realised was irreconcilable with revolutionary political practice and inapplicable in the concrete conditions in which they were situated. The political violence of the youth, which began to explode on the Tamil political scene in the early seventies and took organised forms of revolutionary resistance in the later stages, became a frightening political reality to both the peace-loving conservative Tamil leadership and to the oppressive Sinhala regimes.

The determinant element that hardened the Tamil youth to militancy, defiance and violence was that they were the immediate targets and victims of the racist policies of successive Sinhala governments. The educated youth were confronted with appalling levels of unemployment which offered them nothing other than a bleak future of perpetual despair. The government's discriminatory programme of standardisation and the racist Sinhala Only policy practically closed the doors to higher education and employment.

Plunged into the despair of unemployed existence, frustrated without the possibility of higher education, angered by the imposition of an alien language, the Tamil youth realised that the redemption to their plight lay in revolutionary politics, a politics that should pave the way for a radical and fundamental transformation of their miserable conditions of existence. The only alternative left to the Tamils under the conditions of mounting national oppression, the youth rightly perceived, was none other than a revolutionary armed struggle for the total independence of their nation. Therefore, the radical Tamil youth, while making impassioned demands pressuring the old generation of the Tamil United Front leadership to advocate secession, resorted to revolutionary political violence to express their militant stand.

Political violence

The political violence of the youth in the early seventies should be conceived both as a militant protest to the savage forms of state domination as well as a revolutionary expression and continuation of the national struggle of the Tamils. This youth violence opened up a new dimension in Tamil politics, ushering a new revolutionary epoch in the historical struggle of a nation of people for political independence.

In documenting the historical origin of youth violence in Tamil politics, we should give credit to an organisation that moulded the most militant political activists and created the conditions for the emergence of revolutionary political practice. This organisation was the Tamil Student Federation, which produced the most determined and dedicated youth, whose singleminded devotedness to the cause of national freedom became an inspiration to others. The most outstanding freedom fighter who emerged from this tradition and became a martyr was the youth named Sivakumaran. The earnestness, courage and determination of this young Tamil revolutionary in defying and challenging the authority of the Sinhalese state, particularly the repressive police apparatus, became a great legend. The revolutionary violence by which he kindled the flame of freedom became an inextinguishable fire that began to spread all over Tamil Eelam.

Political violence flared up in the form of bombings, shootings, robberies and attacks on government property. A Sinhalese minister's car was bombed during his visit to the north. An assassination attempt was made on Mr R. Thiyagarajah, a Tamil parliamentarian who betrayed the Tamil cause by supporting the Republican Constitution. An ardent government supporter, Mr Kumarakulasingham, former chairman of the Nallur Village Council, was shot dead. Violent incidents erupted throughout Tamil Eelam on the day the new constitution was passed. Buses were burned, government buildings were bombed and Sinhala national flags were burned.

Confronted with widespread violence, which expressed none other than revolutionary resentment and rebellion against oppression, the state machinery reacted with repression and terror, delegating excessive powers to the police. Empowered by law and encouraged by the ruling elite, the police practised excessive violence indiscriminately against innocent people and primarily against the Tamil youth. The police tyranny manifested in the horrors of torture, imprisonment (without trial) and murders. The most abominable act of police brutality occurred on the night of the last day (10 January 1974) of the Fourth International Conference of Tamil Research held in Jaffna. During this great cultural event – when nearly a hundred thousand Tamil people were spellbound by the eloquent speech of the great Tamil scholar from southern India, professor Naina Mohamed – the grim tragedy struck. Hundreds of Sinhala policemen armed to the teeth launched a well-planned, lightning attack on the spectators with tear gas bombs, batons and rifle butts, which exploded into a gigantic commotion and stampede resulting in the tragic loss of eight lives and hundreds – including women and children – sustaining severe injuries. This event cut a deep wound in the heart of the Tamil nation; it profoundly humiliated the national pride of the Tamil speaking people. The event betrayed the vicious character of the state police, which in the eyes of Tamils became a terrorist instrument of state oppression.

The birth of the Tiger movement

The revolutionary ardour of the Tamil youth, which manifested in the form of indiscriminate outbursts of political violence in the early seventies, sought concrete political expression in an organisational structure built on a revolutionary political theory and practice. Neither the Tamil United Front nor the left movement offered any concrete political venue to the revolutionary potential of the rebellious youth.

The political structure of the Tamil United Front, founded on a conservative bourgeois ideology, could not provide the basis for the articulation of revolutionary politics. It became very clear to the Tamil masses and particularly to the revolutionary youth that the Tamil nationalist leaders, though they fiercely championed the cause of the Tamils, have failed to formulate any concrete practical programme of political action to liberate the oppressed Tamil nation. Having ex- hausted all forms of popular struggle for the last three decades, having been alienated from the power structure of the Sinhala state, the Tamil politicians still clung to parliament to air their disgruntlement, which went unheard, unheeded like vain cries in the wilderness. The strategy of the traditional left parties was to collaborate with the Sinhala capi- talist class and therefore their theoretical perspective was subsumed by the hegemonic ideology of that dominant class, which was none other than chauvinism. This suicidal class collaboration made the left leaders turn a blind eye to the stark realities of national oppression; it made them ignore the revolutionary conditions generated by the Tamil national struggle; it made them incapable of mobilising the revolutionary aspirations of the Tamil militants.

Confronted with this political vacuum and caught up in a revolutionary situation created by the concrete conditions of intolerable national oppression, the Tamil revolutionary youth sought desperately to create a revolutionary political organisation to advance the task of national liberation. It was in this specific political conjuncture that the Tiger movement took its historical birth in 1972. The movement was formed by its present leader and military commander Velupillai Prabhakaran. At the time of its inauguration, the movement called itself the Tamil New Tigers and later, on 5 May 1976, the organisation renamed itself as the Liberation Tigers of Tamil Eelam. From its inception, the Tiger movement took into its ranks the most resolute, the most dedicated, most zealous young revolutionaries.

Structured as an urban guerrilla force, disciplined with an iron will to fight for the cause of national freedom, the Tigers emerged as the armed resistance movement of the oppressed Tamil masses. As a revolutionary liberation movement, it provided a concrete organisational base to the insurrectionary spirit of the rebellious youth and soon established itself as the armed vanguard of the national struggle. The Tigers' commitment to armed struggle as the form of popular mass struggle was undertaken after a careful and cautious appraisal of the objective conditions of the national struggle, with the fullest comprehension of the concrete situation in which the masses of people were presented with no other alternative other than to resort to revolutionary resistance to advance their national cause.

Prabhakaran, the leader of the Tiger movement, is an ardent young revolutionary, born on 26 November 1951 in the coastal town of Valvettiturai, a place famous for its militancy against Sinhala state repression. He was drawn into revolutionary politics when he was sixteen and earned the name "Thamby" [little brother] among co-revolutionaries as he was very young. Prabhakaran represented the aspirations of the rebellious Tamil youth who, having become disenchanted with the failures of non-violent political campaigns, resolved to fight back the barbarous form of state violence perpetrated on their people. Prabhakaran soon organised a politico-military structure which gave an organisational expression to the revolutionary ardour of these militant youth. Showing an extraordinary talent in planning military strategy and tactics and executing them to the amazement of the enemy, Prabhakaran soon became a symbol of Tamil resistance and the Tiger movement he founded became the revolutionary movement to spearhead the Tamil national liberation struggle.

Ideologically bound to the revolutionary theory and practice of Marxism and Leninism, our movement firmly believes that its commitment to armed struggle is not an alternative to mass movement. The revolutionary armed resistance must be sustained and supported by the mobilised masses. The invincible power of the organised masses, we believe, must be activated as the force of popular resistance. Adopting Lenin's teaching that armed struggle "must be ennobled by the enlightening and organising influence of socialism", our movement has chartered its political programme integrating the national struggle with class struggle, defining our ultimate objective as national liberation and socialist revolution. With the conviction that armed struggle is the highest expression of political practice and must be channelled into a process of socialist revolution, the Tiger movement, from its earliest stages, engaged in developing and building political and military bases among the popular masses.

A mandate for secession

The emergence of the Tiger movement marked a new historical epoch in the nature and structure of the Tamil national struggle, extending the dimension of the agitation to popular armed resistance. While our movement was engaged in organising and developing its politico-military structure, great events of extraordinary political significance began to unfold in the Tamil political domain. It was the time when national oppression assumed such severity and harshness that made joint existence between the two nations intolerable and impossible. It was at the peak of this national oppression, when secession became the inevitable political destiny of the Tamil nation, that the Tamil United Front called for a national convention in May 1976 at Vaddukoddai, where a historic resolution was unanimously adopted calling for complete political independence of the Tamil nation. It was at this conference that Tamil United Front changed its name to Tamil United Liberation Front (TULF). The convention condemned the Republican Constitution of 1972, which "has made the Tamils a slave nation ruled by the new colonial masters the Sinhalese who are using the power they usurped to deprive the Tamil nation of its territory, language, citizenship, economic life, opportunities of employment and education, thereby destroying all the attributes of nationhood of the Tamil people". The convention resolved that "restoration and reconstitution of the free, sovereign, secular, socialist state of Tamil Eelam based on the right to self-determination inherent to every nation has become inevitable in order to safeguard the very existence of the Tamil nation in this country".

The general elections of July 1977 became a crucial testing ground for the secessionist cause of the Tamil United Liberation Front. The TULF asked for a clear mandate from the people to wage a national struggle for secession and accordingly the Front explicitly stated in the Manifesto:

> "Hence the Tamil United Liberation Front seeks in the general election the mandate of the Tamil Nation to establish an independent sovereign secular, socialist state of Tamil Eelam that includes all the geographically contiguous areas that have been the traditional homelands of the Tamil speaking people in this country."

The Manifesto further stated:

> "The Tamil Nation must take the decision to establish its sovereignty in its homeland as the basis of its right to self-determination. The only way to announce this decision to the Sinhalese government and to the world is to vote for the Tamil United Liberation Front."

The Manifesto finally pledged:

> "The Tamil speaking representatives who get elected through these votes, while being members of the National State Assembly of Ceylon, will also form themselves into the National Assembly Of Tamil Eelam, which will draft a constitution for the state of Tamil Eelam and to establish the independence of Tamil Eelam by bringing that constitution into operation either by peaceful means or by direct action or struggle."

In reference to the Tamil question, the verdict at the elections was very crucial. It was fought precisely on a decision to secede. In a political sense, it assumed the character of a plebiscite, a public expression of a nation's will. The Tamil speaking people voted overwhelmingly in favour of secession, or rather, the people of Tamil Eelam exercised, through a democratic political practice, their right to self-determination, their right to secede and form an independent state of their own. Thus, the Tamil question assumed a new dimension. It's no longer a question to be resolved by district councils or by federal system, nor by negotiations and pacts. It is no longer a question to bargain for concessions. It has become a question of national self-determination, a question of an inalienable right of a nation of people to decide their own political destiny. The Tamil nation did proclaim its determination to be an independent sovereign state, and this national will was articulated through a popular democratic practice. This was the specific mandate given to the TULF leadership, an authentic irreversible mandate stamped with the popular will, a mandate to establish an independent sovereign socialist state of Tamil Eelam.

The repression and resistance

The general elections of 1977 resulted in a massive victory for the extreme right wing United National Party … The traditional left parties were completely wiped out without a single seat, and the Tamil United Liberation Front, for the first time in Ceylon's political history, became the leading opposition party in parliament. The stage was set for a confrontation: the Tamils demanding secession and separate existence as a sovereign state and the Sinhala racist ruling party seeking absolute state power to dominate and subjugate the will of the Tamil nation to live free. The intensity of this contradiction took its manifest form soon after the elections in a racial holocaust unprecedented in its violence towards the Tamils.

In this island-wide racial conflagration, hundreds of Tamils were mercilessly massacred, millions worth of Tamil property was destroyed and thousands of them made refugees. The state police and the armed forces openly colluded with the hooligans in their gruesome acts of arson, looting, rape and mass murder. Instead of containing the racist violence that was ravaging the whole island, the government leaders made inflammatory statements with racist connotations that added fuel to the fire. It was the Tamil plantation workers who bore the brunt of this racial onslaught. Seventeen thousand of them became refugees and sought asylum in the Tamil areas of the north and east.

The racial horror had a profound impact on Tamil political thinking. While it hardened the militancy of the revolutionary youth, it exposed the political impotence of the Tamil bourgeois leadership, who, having failed to fulfil its pledges to the people, sought a collaborationist strategy to placate the Sinhala leaders. Jayawardene in his Machiavellian shrewdness soon realised that TULF leaders were not serious in their secessionist demand but sought an alternative to deceive the Tamil masses. The real threat of secession, the government thought, arose from the militant Tamil youths who are unappeasable, irreconcilable and committed to the core to the goal of an independent socialist Tamil Eelam. The new regime, therefore, utilised all means to crush the revolutionary youth, the very ground from where the cry for political freedom emanated. The government thus embarked on a ruthless policy of repression, delegating extra powers to the police and military to clamp down on the Tamil youth. Caught up in a revolutionary situation and constantly victimised by the police, the young Tamil revolutionaries were forced to resist the state repression. The dialectic of repression and resistance began to unfold into a deadly national struggle, ushering the armed people's war that opened a new dimension in the freedom movement of the Eelam Tamils.

Tiger movement comes to limelight

On 7 April 1978, a police raiding party headed by the notorious torturer inspector Bastiampillai suddenly surrounded a Tiger training camp deep in the northern jungle and held the guerrillas at gun point. One of our commando leaders, lieutenant Chelvanayagam (alias Aman), tactfully swooped on a police officer, snatched his 5MG and gunned down the police party. Inspector Bastiampillai, sub-inspector Perambalam, police constable Balasingham and police driver Siriwardana were all killed. Our guerrilla unit sustained no casualties. The incident alarmed the government but created euphoria among the Tamils since it signified the first major incident of armed resistance against the repressive state apparatus.

On 25 April, the Tiger movement for the first time officially claimed responsibility for the annihilation of the raiding party and the earlier killings of police officers and Tamil traitors. Thus, the Tiger movement came to limelight announcing itself to the world as the revolutionary resistant movement of the Tamils committed to the goal of national liberation of Tamil Eelam through armed struggle. The Sinhala government reacted swiftly by enacting a law proscribing the Tiger movement. The government also poured into Tamil areas large contingents of armed units for the "Tiger hunt" and brought the Tamil nation under total military occupation.

Having intensified the military repression in Tamil Eelam, Jayawardene introduced a new constitution on 7 September, which bestowed upon him absolute dictatorial executive powers, gave Sinhala language and Buddhist religion extraordinary status, and relegated a second class status to the Tamil language. While the Tamil parliamentary party failed in its duty to register any mass protest, the Tiger movement brought the matter to the attention of the international community by blowing up an AVRO aircraft, the only passenger plane owned by the national airline (Air Ceylon). The incident was a humiliation to the government but boosted the morale of the Tamil freedom movement. The Tigers stepped up the campaign by raiding a government bank (Tinnevely People's Bank) on 5 December, appropriating 1.68 million rupees of state money. In this daring daylight raid, two police officers were shot dead and another was seriously wounded. Our guerrilla fighters escaped without any casualty, taking away the weapons from the enemy.

To stamp out the growing armed resistance, the government took draconian measures. On 20 July 1979, Jayawardene's racist regime enacted the Prevention of Terrorism Act, which contained the most infamous provisions that contravened the very principles of the rule of law and violated the norms of human justice. This notorious law denied trial by jury, enabled the detention of people for a period of eighteen months and allowed confessions extracted under torture as admissible in evidence. Having enacted the law, the government declared a state of emergency in Jaffna, the northern Tamil capital, and dispatched more military units to Tamil areas under the command of brigadier Weeratunga with special instructions to wipe out "terrorism" within six months.

128

Empowered by law and encouraged by the state, the fascist brigadier unleashed military terror unprecedented in its violence. Hundreds of innocent youths were arrested and subjected to barbarous torture, and several of them were shot dead and their bodies were dumped on the roadside. Their oppressive measures caused massive outcry all over the world, and the Terrorism Act brought universal condemnation by the world human rights movements, particularly by the International Commission of Jurists and Amnesty International.

Tigers step up guerrilla campaign

The political events that unfolded since 1981 involved massive genocidal onslaughts on the life and property of the Tamil community and increased guerrilla campaigns of our liberation movement.

On the midnight of 31 May 1981, the Sinhala police went on a wild rampage, burning down the city of Jaffna. This state terrorism exploded into a mad frenzy of arson, looting and murder. Hundreds of shops were burnt to ashes, the Jaffna market square was set in flames. A Tamil newspaper office and Jaffna MP's house were gutted. The most abominable act of cultural genocide was the burning down of the famous Jaffna public library, destroying more than ninety thousand volumes of invaluable literary and historical works, an act that outraged the conscience of the world Tamils. The whole episode was masterminded by two cabinet ministers (Cyril Mathew and Gamini Dissanayake) of Jayawardene's regime, who were in Jaffna during the riots and were supervising the orgy of police violence.

An island-wide racial conflagration flared up again just three months after the burning of Jaffna, a racial onslaught on the Tamils organised by leading members of the government, assisted by the armed forces, and executed by gangs of Sinhala thugs and hooligans. And again our people became the cruel victims of Sinhala racist barbarity; victims of insane sadistic orgy, victims of arson, looting, rape and murder.

Hundreds of our people, including women and children, were slaughtered, thousands of them made homeless and millions worth of Tamil property destroyed. The repetitive pattern of this organised violence that brought colossal damage in terms of life and property to our people signified the genocidal intent underlying this horrid phenomenon. The objective of the chauvinistic ruling class is nothing other than to inflict maximum injury to the Tamils, to terrorise, subjugate and destroy the aspirations of our people for political independence. Yet more and more the oppression intensified, the determination of our people became more and more hardened with an iron will to resist the forces of repression. As the consequence of heightened repression, the resistance of the freedom fighters increased with such a vehemence that it caused the destabilisation of the Sinhala state and disrupted the civil administrative system in Tamil Eelam.

On 2 July 1982, the Tiger guerrillas launched a lightening attack on a police patrolling party at Nelliady, Jaffna, killing four police officers on the spot. Three police personnel were seriously injured.

Another major incident of guerrilla attack that shook the Sinhala police system was the successful raid on the well-guarded Chavakachcheri police station. On the early morning of 27 October, a Tiger guerrilla unit commanded by lieutenant Lucas Charles Antony (alias Aseer) launched a well-planned sudden attack on the police station, killing three police officers and injuring several others. The rest of the police personnel fled in terror. From the police armoury we raided thirty-three pieces of weaponry – nineteen repeater guns, nine 303 rifles, two sub-machine guns, two shot guns and one revolver. Two of our guerrilla members sustained minor injuries. This successful guerrilla raid forced the government to close down almost all the police stations in the north, and the police administrative system became paralysed.

On 18 February 1983, our freedom fighters shot and killed police inspector Wijewardane and his jeep driver Rajapaksa of Point Pedro police station. Inspector Wijewardane is notorious for police repression in that area.

On 4 March at Umaiyalpuram, Paranthan, our guerrilla fighters ambushed an army convoy. In the gun battle that ensued, several army personnel were seriously injured and the rest fled in fear. In that ambush, two armoured cars were damaged.

On 2 April, the Tigers blasted the Jaffna Secretariat building by bombs, just a few hours before a government-organised "security conference" to discuss ways and means to crush the Tiger movement. The blast caused extensive damage to the building and destroyed all state documents. Several government jeeps were set on fire.

On 29 April, the Liberation Tigers assassinated three prominent supporters of the ruling United National Party on the same day, as a warning to all Tamil traitors who supported the racist government. Two of them were UNP candidates for the local elections (F.V. Ratnasingham of Point Pedro and S.S. Muthiah of Chavakachcheri) and the other, S.S. Rajaratnam, a long time UNP supporter and the bodyguard of UNP's Jafina organiser K. Ganeshalingam. As a direct consequence of this action, all the Tamil UNP candidates withdrew from the elections, and several Tamils resigned from the ruling party.

Tigers' political campaign succeeds

Responding to a mass campaign launched by our movement, the majority of the Tamil people living predominately in the northern province staged a mass boycott of local elections on 18 May 1983.

Such a mass boycott of elections, unprecedented in the political history of the Tamils, constitutes a great political and propaganda victory for the Tiger movement. The TULF, which defied the Tiger appeal, suffered an insulting humiliation and irreparably damaged its political image when 90 percent of the voters in the north rejected the party's appeal to vote. The boycott was called by the Tigers, who, for the first time, launched an effective popular campaign appealing to the people to shun the local government elections as a mark of disapproval and rejection of the racist state system that has imposed a reign of terror and repression against the Tamils. V. Prabhakaran, chairman and the military commander of the Tiger movement, in a statement widely circulated among the people, called upon the Tamils to "reject the civil administrative machinery of the Sri Lankan state terrorists and join the popular armed struggle directed towards national emancipation". He also accused the reactionary bourgeois political party, the Tamil United Liberation Front, of functioning as agents of the Sinhala racist regime and utilising the slogan of "national freedom" to win the elections.

On the day of elections, just before the voting started, time bombs planted by our movement exploded at five polling booths in the Tamil city of Jaffna, causing panic and havoc among the armed forces. On the same day, an hour before the polling ended, Liberation Tiger guerrillas opened fire with machine guns on the army and police units guarding a polling booth at Nallur, Jaffna, killing an army corporal and seriously wounding a soldier and two policemen. As a consequence of guerrilla attacks, the government imposed a state of national emergency.

Reasons for the recent holocaust

The causality that underlies the recent holocaust [Black July] is manifold. It is absurd to assume that our guerrilla ambush on the midnight of 23 July 1983, which killed fourteen Sinhala soldiers and seriously wounded several others, precipitated the calamity. Riots had already exploded at Trincomalee weeks before the guerrilla ambush. Aided by the military, masses of Sinhala hooligans went on a wild rampage at Trincomalee, massacring innocent Tamil people and burning down their houses. Under the cover of emergency and curfew, the military openly colluded with the Sinhala vandals in an orgy of arson, looting and murders.

An all-out genocidal assault on the Tamils living in Colombo has been pre-planned by Sinhala fascist groups led by leading members of the ruling party. The recent outburst, unprecedented in its destructive horror, is therefore certainly an open manifestation of a genocidal programme hatched by the fascist leadership as the Hitlerian "final solution" to the Tamil national question.

There are two basic reasons for the ruling Sinhala bourgeoisie to let loose a genocidal repression on Tamils. Firstly, to divert the mass attention from a deepening economic crisis brought about by a dependent neo-colonial economy which has reduced the Sri Lankan government as a perpetual beggar to Western imperialist aid-giving agencies. The popular resentment that has been accumulating from massive inflation and mass unemployment as a consequence of a disastrous economic policy has been constantly diverted and channelled as anti-Tamil hysteria. Secondly, the massacre of Tamils on a genocidal scale, which the Sinhala fascist ruling class always conceived as the only solution to the national question. Mass killings and massive destruction of property, these fascists wrongly assumed, may humble the Tamils and wipe out the Tamil national freedom struggle.

PART THREE: THEORETICAL AND POLITICO-MILITARY OBJECTIVES

Our theoretical guide to the national question

The principal determinant factor that propelled the dynamics of national friction leading to this inevitable choice of political independence was none other than national oppression. Therefore, in the study of the Tamil Eelam national question, oppression – that is, the oppression of a big nation against a small nation perpetrated within the power structure of a unitary state – becomes the crucial element for a theoretical analysis as well as for a political strategy.

Positing the problem within the theoretical discourse of Marxism, we hold that Lenin's theoretical elucidations and political strategies offer an adequate basis for a precise formulation of this question. Lenin's exposition of the concept of self-determination, which deals primarily with a nation's right to secession and statehood, is adopted here as a theoretical guide to provide a concrete presentation of the Tamil national question.

Our reliance on Lenin's formulations is determined by the fact that neither Marx nor Engels nor any other theoretician offers a systematic theory with a concrete political strategy for proletarian praxis in relation to the national question. Indisputably, Lenin's works will stand as a theoretical and political paradigm in this domain, engaging the problems in manifold aspects. Situating the question within the theoretical framework of historical materialism, providing a historico-economic analysis, Lenin advances a correct proletarian perspective on the national question, interrelating the national struggle with proletarian class struggle. His analysis exposes the limitations and bankruptcy of bourgeois democracy and the dangers of extreme bourgeois nationalism. Lenin firmly held that the non-recognition or rejection of the problems of national minorities will deeply affect the working class movement and obstruct the proletarian struggle for socialist revolution.

While taking Lenin's discourse as our guide, we are not blind to the fact that every national struggle must be situated within the context of its own concrete historical conditions. The liberation struggle of the Tamil Eelam nation demanding political independence, the historical conjunctures of which we have already outlined, arose primarily from the contradictions of national oppression and therefore must be confined to the theoretical specifications and political implications of that nation's right to secession. Within this context, many questions are posed. Whether the oppressed Tamil nation has the right to secede; whether the right of that nation to self-determination contravenes the socialist principle of proletarian internationalism; under what political and economic conditions of oppression will a nation opt for secession; whether such a decision to secede and the struggle for political independence will serve the interests of the class struggle of both the oppressed and the oppressor nations; whether the struggle for political independence has the revolutionary potentiality to promote proletarian revolution and socialist transformation of the oppressed Tamil social formation; what kind of political strategy can best serve the class interests of the proletariat of the oppressed as well as the oppressor nations, a strategy which has to be adopted by the Marxist revolutionaries of the oppressor nation who are caught between a progressive struggle of an oppressed nation and a reactionary bourgeois nationalism of the oppressor nation. These problems are raised and hotly debated within the context of the Tamil national question. The debates and arguments enmeshed with vague generalisations and loose conceptualisations have created so much confusion and controversy that a clarity and a correct perspective on this issue has become absolutely essential.

Self-determination and secession

The Tamil nation is a historically constituted social formation possessing all the basic elements that are usually assembled to define a concrete characterisation of a nation. Yet a definition as to what constitutes a nation is theoretically unnecessary since we can precisely formulate our issue within the Leninist conceptual framework of the self-determination of nations.

The concept of self-determination needs a precise and clear definition. Such a clarification is vital to our national question, since some of the so-called Leninists in Sri Lanka are confused on this basic concept. The most ridiculous misrepresentation and misconceptuali-sation of this concept arises from a position in which the right of the Tamil nation to self-determination is given recognition while opposing secession. Attempting to show a radical face as revolutionaries, these political opportunists are proclaiming that the Tamil speaking people as an oppressed nation has the right to self-determination, but they do not have the right to secession. It is precisely on this position one finds a calculated distortion of a clearly defined concept. Lenin's texts on the national question constantly reiterate the definition that the self-determination of nations is nothing but secession and the formation of an independent state. To quote a couple of examples:

> "Consequently, if we want to grasp the meaning of self-determination of nations, not by juggling with legal definitions, or 'inventing' abstract definitions, but by examining the historico-economic conditions of the national movements, we must inevitably reach the conclusion that the self-determination of nations means the political separation of these nations from alien national bodies and the formation of an independent national state." (Lenin, *The right of nations to self-determination*)

Again, in the same theoretical essay Lenin writes:

> "Self-determination of nations in the Marxist programme cannot, from a historico-economic point of view, have any other meaning than political self-determination, state independence, and the formation of a national state."

Thus, Lenin offers a precise definition. The right of nations to self-determination in his formulation means the right of an oppressed nation to secede from the oppressor nation and form an independent national state. Therefore, those who pretend to recognise the right of the oppressed Tamil nation to self-determination and argue such a right does not embody the freedom to secede, are neither Marxists nor Leninists but chauvinists parading under socialist slogans. To characterise these pseudo-socialists in Lenin's own words:

> "A socialist in any of the oppressor nations who does not recognise and does not struggle for the right of the oppressed nations to self-determination (i.e. for the right to secession) is in reality a chauvinist, not a socialist."

The freedom of an oppressed nation to secede in Lenin's theoretical analysis is advanced, on one level, as a universal socialist principle of workers' democracy, a cornerstone of what Lenin calls "consistent democracy". On a different level, the struggle of an oppressed nation to secession is seen as a revolutionary ground for mass action, a ground for a proletarian onslaught on the bourgeoisie. Therefore, the political genius of Lenin situates this struggle of the oppressed nations within the realms of socialist democracy and proletarian revolution. It is precisely within these two spheres we wish to situate the Tamil national question to elucidate the progressive and revolutionary character of this independence struggle.

Inalienable right of a nation

In championing the right of secession and articulating the principle of self-determination in the national, democratic programme, Lenin sparked off a violent theoretical controversy among his co-revolutionaries. Whether such a right will lead to disintegration and fragmentation of smaller states, whether the freedom to secede contradicts the Marxian principle of proletarian internationalism, were questions raised against his theses on the national question. These questions and Lenin's consistent defence of this position are important to us because it is precisely these questions that are hurled against the Tamil demand for secession.

The freedom of secession should not be confused with the reactionary bourgeois category of "separatism", which is sometimes utilised to undermine the genuine democratic struggle of the oppressed Tamil nation. The freedom of secession articulated within the concept of self-determination exclusively implies an inalienable right of a nation of people to agitate for political independence from the oppressor nation. This complete freedom to agitate for secession is a right, which can be exercised under conditions of intolerable oppression. Therefore, the recognition of this right to secession, Lenin repeatedly argued, is vital to prevent national friction arising out of a big nation's chauvinism, a right that upholds the complete equality of nations, a right, which if violated will lead to national hostility and the fragmentation of nations. It is here Lenin advances the dialectical principle that in order to ensure unity there must be freedom to separate. He even argued that freedom to divorce will not cause the disintegration of the family. Therefore, Lenin rigorously held he was not advocating a doctrine of separatism but advancing a higher principle of socialist democracy in which absolute freedom should be accorded to a nation of people to secede under any conditions of oppression. To quote him in this context:

"Specifically, this demand for political democracy implies complete freedom to agitate for secession ... This demand therefore is not the equivalent of a demand for separation, fragmentation and the formation of small states. It implies only a consistent expression of struggle against all national oppression." (Lenin, *The socialist revolution and the right of nations to self-determination*)

Proletarian internationalism

Marxist political praxis certainly advances proletarian internationalism, but at the same time gives fullest recognition to the revolutionary character and the historical legitimacy of national movements. The principle of nationality, or rather, the phenomenon of nationalism itself, in Marxist discourse is characterised as an historically inevitable political phenomenon in bourgeois society. For Marx, nationalism is historically prior to proletarian internationalism. Proletarian revolutions in the advanced capitalist social formations, Marx foresaw, will generate the progressive forces of internationalism towards the gradual structuration and consolidation of a world socialist society. Lenin, who saw the historical unfolding of the great socialist revolution, became an ardent champion of proletarian internationalism, since he rightly believed that only the revolutionary power of a united international proletariat can challenge the structure of dominance of world capitalism. Therefore, we find in Lenin's texts a constant emphasis on the necessity of the solidarity of the working classes of all nations to mobilise to fight against the hegemony of international capital.

Yet, on the other hand, we find Lenin as a fierce champion of the oppressed; he fought vigorously against all forms of oppression. He correctly perceived that national oppression is the enemy of the class struggle and, without the emancipation of the oppressed, proletarian solidarity of the oppressed and the oppressor nations is unattainable. That is why Lenin firmly held that proletarian internationalism demands that the proletariat of the oppressor nation should grant the right to self-determination (i.e. the right to secession) to the oppressed nation:

> "The proletariat must struggle against the enforced retention of oppressed nations within the bounds of the given state, which means that they must fight for the right to self-determination. The proletariat must demand freedom of political separation for the colonies and nations oppressed by 'their own' nation. Otherwise, the internationalism of the proletariat would be nothing but empty words, neither confidence nor class solidarity would be possible between the workers of the oppressed and the oppressor nations." (Lenin, *The socialist revolution and the right of nations to self-determination*)

The right of nations to self-determination does not contravene the socialist principle of proletarian internationalism. On the contrary, as Lenin has shown, the recognition of this right is a fundamental necessity to advance internationalism. It will amount to chauvinism and political opportunism to preach the noble ideals of internationalism to a nation of people caught up in a liberation struggle against the oppression of the bigger dominant nation.

Intolerable oppression and inevitable secession

We are now approaching the most crucial stage of our discussion on the Tamil Eelam national question. That is, under what political and economic conditions of oppression a nation will opt for secession, and whether such a decision to secede and the struggle for national independence will serve the interests of the class struggle of both the oppressed and oppressor nations. An elucidation of these issues is vital for a theoretical comprehension and for a political strategy for prole-tarian revolutionaries in Sri Lanka who are confronted with a national struggle of an oppressed nation which has chosen the path of secession.

The determinant factors behind the Tamils' decision to secede and form a state of their own, as we have pointed out earlier, are the historical conditions of intolerable national oppression. The cumulative effects of this multi-dimensional oppression made joint existence unbearable. The contradictions that emanated from national friction made a political rupture inevitable. Thrown into the painful dilemma of political isolation and economic deprivation and threatened with an annihilation of their ethnic identity, the Tamil speaking people of Eelam nation had no other alternative but to opt for secession. Under intensified conditions of national oppression, a decision to secede and fight for political independence is not only a correct action but also a revolutionary move which will serve the interests of the class struggle. Lenin says:

> "From their daily experience the masses know perfectly well the value of geographical and economic ties and the advantages of a big state. They will therefore resort to secession only when national oppression and national friction make joint life absolutely intolerable and hinder any and all economic intercourse. In that case, the interests of capitalist development and of the freedom of the class struggle will be best served by secession." (Lenin, *The right of nations to self-determination*)

Within the Leninist perspective, we can safely hold that the decision of the oppressed Tamil nation to secede from the oppressor nation was necessary and historically inevitable because of the extreme conditions of oppression, the nature and form of which we have outlined in the early parts of this document. The question that can be posed now is whether the Tamil struggle for political independence will serve the interests of the class struggle of the oppressed and oppressor nations.

The role of the progressives of the oppressor nation

Marx, who supported the Irish national movement, called upon the English working classes to fight for the liberation of Ireland, which he considered an oppressed colony under England. He firmly held that the liberation of Ireland was a necessity and an essential condition for the emancipation of the English working classes. He asserted that no nation can be free while it practises oppression against another country. The writings of Marx and Lenin on the national question announce a very important political truth, that national oppression would inevitably hold back and divide the working classes of the oppressor nation. It is through oppression and through the hegemony of a national chauvinistic ideology that the ruling bourgeoisie exerts dominance and power over the working masses of the oppressor nation. Marx wrote:

> "It is (Britain's oppression of Ireland) the secret of the impotence of the English working class, despite their organisation. It is the secret by which the capitalist class maintains its power." (Marx's Letter to Meyer and Vogt, 9 April 1870)

Lenin took Marx as his guide on the national question when he wrote:

> "Our model will always be Marx, who, after living in Britain for decades and becoming half-English, demanded freedom and national independence for Ireland in the interests of the socialist movement of the British workers." (Lenin, *On the national pride of the great Russians*)

We advocate that the progressives and revolutionaries of the oppressor nation (in this case, the Sinhala nation) who uphold the proletarian praxis of Marxism and Leninism should follow the strategy advanced by these great revolutionary teachers and give unconditional, unrelenting support to the freedom struggle of the oppressed Tamil nation. Such a political strategy can only serve the interests of the class struggle of both the oppressed and the oppressor nation, since the ruling Sinhala bourgeoisie has been reinforcing a chauvinistic ideological hegemony and has been practising a vicious form of national oppression with the motive of dividing and weakening the working class movement of Sri Lanka. To break this bourgeois ideological hegemony and to unite the proletariat of the oppressor nation, the revolutionary Marxists in the south should advance an ideological battle supporting most resolutely the right of the oppressed Tamil nation to secession. Such strategy requires a profound political education of the masses on the democratic rights of the oppressed nation. As Lenin said, "The masses [must] be systematically educated to champion – most resolutely, consistently, boldly and in a revolutionary manner" – the right of nations to self-determination. Such an ideological struggle on the part of the Sinhala progressives is essential to raise the level of political consciousness of the Sinhala proletariat to understand and accept the legitimacy of the Tamil cause. It is precisely this lack of political consciousness that draws Sinhala masses into anti-Tamil racial violence and prevents the development of a proletarian class consciousness.

Proletarian revolutionaries committed to the task of socialist revolution should seek to understand the revolutionary potential of mass movements. The national liberation struggle of the oppressed Tamil nation has such revolutionary potential. The failure on the part of the Sinhalese progressives to chart a political programme with the fullest comprehension of the objective and subjective conditions of that struggle will be a great setback to the class struggle of the Sinhala nation.

The most important political truth to be grasped in this historical situation is that only the national emancipation of the oppressed Tamil nation will enable the working masses of the oppressor nation to free themselves from the shackles of bourgeois chauvinism and mobilise them against the state power. The liberated socialist Tamil Eelam would be a revolutionary ally of the oppressed Sinhala masses to fight and destroy the bourgeois state apparatus.

National struggle and class struggle

The theoretical perspective of historical materialism necessitates the investigation of any national movement in relation to the historical development of world capitalism. The nationalism of the European nation states arose with the collapse of feudalism and the transitions to capitalism, with the unification of markets and the revolutionary development of productive forces leading to the birth of a new bourgeois class. The ascendancy of the bourgeoisie and bourgeois nationalism led to the oppression and exploitation of other nations. The advanced stage of capitalist development gave rise to monopoly capitalism, which took the global form of imperialism. The imperialist penetration and its form of oppression produced determinant effects on the mode of production of the peripheral formations. Separating the direct producers from their means of production, creating a mass of free labourers, these effects generated the dynamics of the capitalist mode in the penetrated societies. The development of the productive forces in the capitalist mode led to the organisation of the proletariat as a revolutionary class force.

The imperialist penetration not only generated the mechanisms of capitalist development but also shifted the national struggles to the peripheral social formations. In this context, the nature of nationalism, the national struggle and the class relations in the national movements of the Third World countries must be viewed in relation to the transformations in the expanding capitalist economy, its global effects, its structural relations with developing peripheral capitalism. The world hegemony and the development of the revolutionary proletarian classes within the space of imperialist dominance have changed the structure and character of the contemporary national struggles of the Third World. The so-called progressive national bourgeoisie has lost its revolutionary character to advance the national struggle as a democratic social force. The historical conjuncture of global capitalism has eliminated all progressive elements of the national bourgeoisie, its historical role in the national revolution has shifted to the revolutionary proletariat.

Such structural transformation in the class elements has necessitated a revolutionary socialist strategy interrelating the class struggle with national liberation struggle under the leadership of the revolutionary proletariat, a strategy to advance the class struggle along with the national liberation struggle both against the indigenous bourgeoisie and international capitalism. This political objective of our movement is to advance the national struggle along with the class struggle, or rather, our fundamental objective is national emancipation and socialist transition of our social formation.

The politico-military strategy

The politico-military strategy of our liberation movement is devised in accordance with the specific concrete conditions of our oppressed nation. We are committed, since the inception of our movement, to an armed revolutionary struggle to achieve our ultimate objective, i.e. the establishment of an independent sovereign socialist state of Tamil Eelam. Our strategy aims at the organisation and politicisation of the broad masses of Tamil Eelam towards a popular war of national liberation and socialist revolution. Our total strategy therefore integrates both the national struggle and class struggle, interlinking both nationalism and socialism into a revolutionary project aimed at liberating our people both from national oppression and from the exploitation of man by man. This strategy aims to fuse the progressive patriotic feelings of the broad masses with proletarian class consciousness to accelerate the process of national emancipation and socialist transition of our social formation.

The military objective of our national movement is not simply confined to a confrontation with the armed forces of the oppressive regime, nor is our commitment to revolutionary resistance an alternative to mass movement. Our revolutionary organisation holds the view that armed resistance, to be a genuine mode of popular struggle, must be sustained and supported by the wider sections of broad masses.

Since the banning of our movement, we have been functioning as a revolutionary underground, with political and military cells all over Tamil Eelam. We have chosen urban guerrilla warfare as the effective mode of armed struggle after a careful and cautious appraisal of the specific conditions of our national situation. Our guerrilla units live with the people, sustained by the people, like the fish in the sea. Our military units are always based in Tamil Eelam and continue to struggle heroically as the armed vanguard of our oppressed people. Our freedom fighters are armed political militants, political agents with a mission of liberating our people from all modes of oppression and exploitation. Our guerrilla fighters are conscious of the revolutionary dictum that politics guides the gun. By the consistent hard work of our political cadres, our movement has recruited into its ranks peasants, workers, students and revolutionary intellectuals and we are fast growing into a mass national movement.

Since the recent genocidal onslaught, vast sections of the popular masses have been rallying behind our liberation organisation since we constitute the most powerful, well-organised fighting force in Tamil Eelam. Because of growing popular support, our politico-military strategy is now projected in transforming our protracted guerrilla warfare into a people's war of national liberation. The process involves massive expansion of our guerrilla units into a people's army of liberation, a process in which vast sections of our people will be drawn into a mass armed struggle.

The effect of our prolonged and very intensifying armed resistance on the morale of the Sinhala soldiers and on the racist state system as a whole is devastating. Unable to contain an effective guerrilla warfare sustained by the entire Tamil people, the morale of the Sinhala army has been shattered. There has been a heavy erosion of discipline among the Sinhala soldiers, and there were cases of mass desertions. The Sinhala soldiers are young, inexperienced, paid servants of the state, who live in an alien territory unwanted and abjectly hated by the people; who live in constant terror of an unseen enemy who will strike at any moment, at any place; who feel no moral or spiritual value in sacrificing life for a war of hatred masterminded by the ruling elite of his nation. We are confident that the time is not far away when we will be able to drive this frightened shaky mercenary army from our motherland.

The effect of our armed struggle on the state system and the economic structure is disastrous. The civil administration of the Sinhala state in Tamil Eelam has been paralysed; political institutions have become defunct; the state system as a whole is destabilised; a state of anarchy is fast developing in the Sinhala nation, and a crisis is brewing up in the government itself. The island's economy is in shambles, primarily due to the cost of sustaining a prolonged guerrilla war and owing to the chaos of perpetual racial violence. The July 1983 racial upheaval has effectively destroyed the entire economic infrastructure of the capital. The fires of hatred unleashed against our people by the Sinhala ruling class have gutted to ashes the very foundations of the island's economy. Sri Lanka has now become a sick man of South Asia – weak, fragile, yet seething with hatred, the venom of which will bring the final disaster.

Our appeal to the progressive world

On several fronts of the world today, a revolutionary war is being fought, a war between two historically antagonistic forces, the oppressed and the oppressor. Our liberation struggle as an oppressed nation is an integral part of this international war, a war of the revolutionaries against the reactionary forces of oppression – the forces of imperialism, neo-colonialism, Zionism and racism. Though each liberation struggle has its own historical specificity and its unique conditions, in their essence they articulate a universal historical aspiration of humankind to be free from all systems of oppression and exploitation. In this context, the Tamil Eelam national struggle is similar in content to that of the Palestinian, Namibian or South African people's struggle, or any struggle of the oppressed people based on their right to self-determination.

In conclusion, we appeal to all progressive forces and revolutionary movements of the world to recognise our people's right to self-determination and give unrelenting support and solidarity to the armed revolutionary struggle of our liberation movement. We, the Liberation Tigers, wish to express our support and solidarity to all revolutionary liberation struggles of the oppressed masses of the world.

RESOURCES

Books on Tamil Eelam

Adele Ann Balasingham, *The will to freedom: an inside view of Tamil resistance*

Adele Ann Balasingham, *Women fighters of Liberation Tigers*

Anton Balasingham, *War and peace: armed struggle and peace efforts of Liberation Tigers*

Malaravan, *War journey: diary of a Tamil Tiger*

Murugar Gunasingham, *The Tamil Eelam liberation struggle: state terrorism and ethnic cleansing (1948-2009)*

N. Malathy, *A fleeting moment in my country: the last years of the LTTE de-facto state*

N. Malathy, *Tamil female civil space: its evolution and decline in Tamil Eelam*

S. Edwin Savundra, *War Diary from Jaffna*

Satchi Ponnambalam, *Sri Lanka: the national question and the Tamil liberation struggle*

Sehchudar Gemini, *Structures of Tamil Eelam: a handbook*

Trevor Grant, *Sri Lanka's secrets: how the Rajapaksa regime gets away with murder*

Other books

Karl Marx, *The communist manifesto*

Michael Löwy, *Fatherland or mother earth? Essays on the national question*

Vladimir Lenin, *The right of nations to self-determination*

Websites

Adayaalam centre for policy research: adayaalam.org

Journalists for Democracy in Sri Lanka: jdslanka.org

People for Equality and Relief in Lanka: pearlaction.org

Tamil nation: tamilnation.co/tamileelam.htm

Other resources

Callum Macrae, *No Fire Zone* (documentary film)

Permanent Peoples' Tribunal on Sri Lanka final judgement (available at ptsrilanka.org)

Phil Miller, *Britain's dirty war against the Tamil people – 1979-2009* (available at ptsrilanka.org)